IMAGES OF AMERICA

ENTERTAINMENT
IN AUGUSTA AND THE CSRA

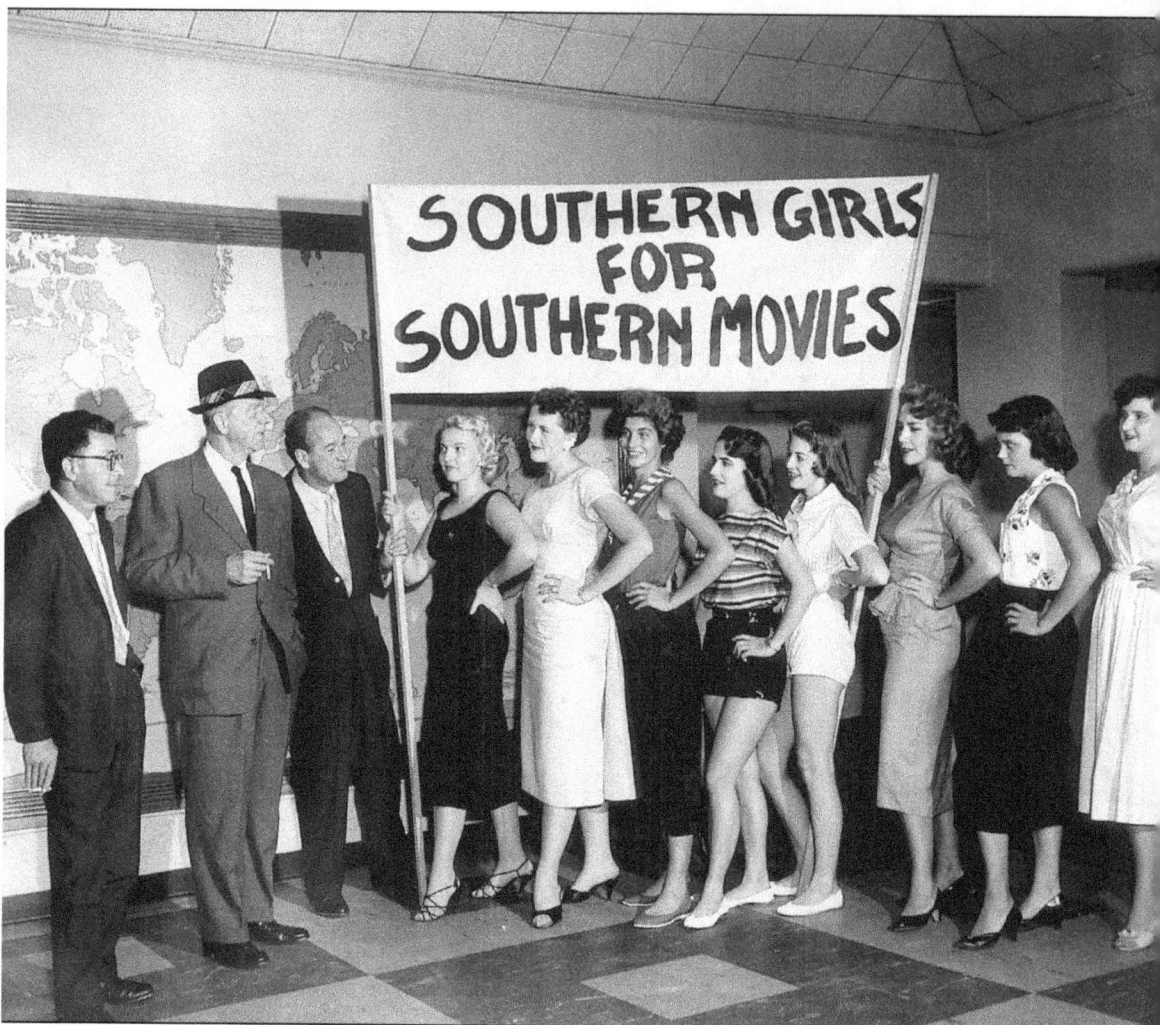

(*on the cover*) **ERSKINE CALDWELL.** This photo was staged on July 25, 1957, at Bush Field airport for the benefit of novelist Erskine Caldwell, second from left, to "protest" the few female roles in the movie version of Mr. Caldwell's novel *God's Little Acre*. Shown, from left to right, are movie producer Sidney Harmon, Caldwell, movie director Anthony Mann, and "protestors" Barbara Bailey, Ann Lane Ford, Faye Griffin, Evelyn Stripling, Gloria Thurmond, Heady Hill, Elaine Black, and Elaine Day. Mr. Caldwell, who grew up in Wrens, Georgia, saw his first published writing in *The Jefferson Reporter* in Wrens. He was also a sports news correspondent for *The Augusta Chronicle*. His lifetime work of more than 60 titles included *Tobacco Road*. Caldwell's first novel, *The Bastard*, was published in October of 1929. His father, Rev. Ira S. Caldwell, also a writer for the *Chronicle*, is buried in Wrens. (Photo by Morgan Fitz, courtesy Fitz-Symms Studio.)

IMAGES OF AMERICA

ENTERTAINMENT
IN AUGUSTA AND THE CSRA

Don "Ramblin'" Rhodes with foreword by Brenda Lee

ARCADIA
PUBLISHING

Published by Arcadia Publishing
Charleston, South Carolina

Library of Congress Control Number: 2003117179

For all general information, please contact Arcadia Publishing:
Telephone 843-853-2070
Fax 843-853-0044
E-mail sales@arcadiapublishing.com
For customer service and orders:
Toll-Free 1-888-313-2665

Visit us on the Internet at www.arcadiapublishing.com

BEAUTY AND THE BEAST. Julia Foley is "Beauty" and Peter Powlus is the "Beast" in an original interpretation of the classic fairytale presented by the Augusta Ballet Company in March of 1990. (Photo by Walt Unks; Courtesy *The Augusta Chronicle*.)

CONTENTS

BRENDA LEE AT 11. In late March of 1956 Brenda Lee first performed on the nationally-televised *Ozark Jubilee* television show hosted by *Grand Ole Opry* star Red Foley. Miss Lee had been discovered by Foley only a few days earlier on February 23, 1956, when allowed to be a guest artist on his show in Augusta's Bell Auditorium. It also was in Augusta that she changed her name from Brenda Mae Tarpley to Brenda Lee. (Courtesy author's collection.)

SUPERSTAR BRENDA LEE. Born in the charity ward of Atlanta's Henry Grady Hospital, Brenda Lee went from living in a small box house on Lionel Street off Gordon Highway in Augusta to performing for Queen Elizabeth II. She has sold more than 100 million recordings, including such giant hits as "I'm Sorry," "Sweet Nothin's," "Break It To Me Gently," "All Alone Am I," "As Usual," "Am I Losing You?," "Jingle Bell Rock," and "Rockin' Around The Christmas Tree." She has been inducted into the Georgia Music Hall of Fame, the Country Music Association Hall of Fame, and the Rock and Roll Hall of Fame. (Courtesy MCA Records.)

6

FOREWORD

At age nine, "Brenda Lee" was booked in August 1954 to debut on Channel 12's (WRDW-TV) *Peach Blossom Special* program in Augusta. My bopping Hank Williams tunes seemed to fit right in with the musical climate, and, to my delight, I was an immediate hit with *Peach Blossom Special* viewers.

On February 23, 1956, local radio personality Peanut Faircloth was hired to emcee a big country show in Bell Auditorium. The headliner was Red Foley, one of the biggest superstars in country music.

Peanut took me to meet him and also asked the show's promoter if I could sing a couple of songs. Amazingly, the organizers agreed to put me on the program. I sang "Jambalaya," and after I finished, Mr. Foley ran over and picked me up in his arms and hugged me.

As if that wasn't enough, I was offered cast membership on Mr. Foley's national television program, *The Ozark Jubilee*, in Springfield, Missouri. Our whole family celebrated by attending the debut performance of Elvis Presley in Augusta a few weeks later on March 20, 1956, where I met him backstage.

Without the people in Augusta and their kindness and belief in me, without my fateful meeting there with Red Foley, I never would have had the career I've had. There's no question in my mind about that.

Over the many years since, I couldn't have been more thankful and proud to be invited to return for performances at the Bell Auditorium. Augusta and its people will forever hold a special place in my heart.

It's not surprising then that Augustan Don Rhodes has been a dear friend of mine for 30 years. Don and I first met in 1974 at the Festival of Music show in Bell Auditorium, where I was performing alongside greats Chet Atkins, Boots Randolph, and Floyd Cramer.

Since then, I've crossed paths with Don many times, both personally and professionally. I have great respect for his work and for his support and love of our entertainment industry.

Thank you, Don, for this wonderful celebration of Augusta. You've been a great friend, and I feel blessed to have you in my life.

—Brenda Lee

ADVERTISEMENT FROM
SEPTEMBER 1954.

Marrh Theatre

North Augusta   Phone 5-3104
Box Office Opens 6:45 p. m.

On Our Stage

AT 9 P. M.
IN PERSON

Pee Wee Devore

and

The Atomic Rangers

Featuring
LITTLE BRENDA LEE
with

CURLEY COLLINS, M. C.

ALSO, ON OUR SCREEN

"THE STAR"

With Bette Davis, Sterling Hayden
At 7:10 and 9:30
—CARTOON—

7

PREFACE

For more than 40 years, ever since my senior year in high school, I have been writing about entertainers. And for the past 20, I have been inundating my life partner, Eddie Smith; my weekly workout buddy, Duncan Wheale; and my co-workers, family, and other friends with stories about Augusta entertainment history. They often have asked when I was going to commit those stories to paper.

I never would have attempted this book without the encouragement and continued support of Billy and Will Morris, CEO and president, respectively, of Morris Communications Company; Julian Miller, president, and Dennis Sodomka, executive editor, of *The Augusta Chronicle*; Jo Ann Hoffman, my Morris corporate communications department boss and friend; and Reginald Wells, my past department boss and friend.

I'm also thankful for technical expertise and advice provided by Robert Symms, Jeff Barnes, Sean Moores, Tami Roose, Belinda Thomas, Leeann Huston, Vince Bertucci, Rhonda Hollimon, John O'Shea, Joseph Lee III, Carrie Adamson, and Kirk Baxley.

Gordon Blaker, curator of the Augusta Museum of History, steered me to Arcadia books and to its regional publisher, Augusta native Katie White, and for that I always will be grateful to both of them.

My family, especially my father, Ollen Rhodes; his wife, Jean; my brothers, Larry Rhodes, Doug Spence, and Mike Spence; and my sisters, Linda Rhodes, Jan Harris, and Ann Holland, have always been there for me, as was my late mother, Ella Sampert Rhodes, who gave me my love of music.

Thanks also to my longtime friend Brenda Lee, who has been such a joy and privilege to know; all the readers of my newspaper and magazine articles and "Ramblin' Rhodes" column; and, finally, thanks to the countless number of Augusta area entertainers, whose accomplishments I can honor with this book.

—Don Rhodes

One

EARLY ENTERTAINMENT OFFERINGS

Probably the single most momentous occasion for Augusta's early entertainment offerings happened when music teacher Claude Simon, formerly of Savannah, staged a concert of vocal and instrumental music at the house of Emanuel Wambersie on May 1, 1787. That apparently was the first formal entertainment offering in Augusta at which an admission fee was charged (10 shillings). It also must have been the first fund-raising event in Augusta since the concert was to raise money to buy musical instruments for Simon's students.

By June of 1790, two talented women, apparently from the theater in Richmond, Virginia—Mrs. Ann Robinson and Miss Susannah Wall—were presenting vocal and theatrical offerings in Augusta, and by July, the "Dramatic Society" (supposedly Augusta's first arts group) was formed.

And that is how organized entertainment in Augusta began.

EMANUEL WAMBERSIE. The first documented professional entertainment in Augusta took place at 7 p.m. on Tuesday, May 1, 1787 at the house of Belgian-born Emanuel Wambersie, whose home was by the Savannah River on Bay Street near Fourth. Wambersie—who in 1795 would marry Ann Phoebe Charlton, first cousin to Francis Scott Key—eventually became a judge in McIntosh County (Darien is now the county seat) and the U.S. Consul to Rotterdam in the Netherlands. (Drawing courtesy Gemeente Rotterdam.)

ELEPHANT POWER. The very first elephant known to be shown in America was exhibited in Augusta "at the house of Mr. Walter Leigh, near the ferry," in mid-May of 1799. The female elephant, weighing about 3,500 pounds, had been bought for $10,000 and brought into New York on April 13, 1796. Elephants have remained popular with Augusta area circus fans such as 35-year-old "Pete," here helping in September of 1989 to raise the big top tent of the Clyde Beatty-Cole Bros. Circus. (Photo by Blake Madden; Courtesy *The Augusta Chronicle*.)

EQUESTRIAN CIRCUS. Horses were important to early area residents as transportation and farm power, but they also were a source of entertainment, such as this Equestrian Circus presented "Tuesdays, Wednesdays and Saturdays" in Augusta in May 1801. The circus presentations would become more and more diverse in the early 1800s, with tumbling by "Mr. Sully" and tightrope walking by "Mr. Placide" in July of 1808; an exhibition of a lion, tiger, camel, leopard, ostriches, and panthers showed in October of 1830 and a giraffe in December of 1838. (Courtesy *The Augusta Chronicle and Gazette of the State*.)

Equeſtrian Circus.

Meſſrs. LANGLEY & Co.

Have the honor to inform the ladies and gentlemen of Auguſta and its vicinity,

That THIS EVENING, May 9,

WILL BE PERFORMED

Several new and aſtoniſhing Feats of Horſemanſhip,

Never before performed here by the Equeſtrian company.

☞ Days of performances— Tueſdays, Wednefdays and Saturdays.

(right) LAURA KEENE. One of the last persons President Abraham Lincoln saw alive was actress Laura Keene, as he watched her acting troupe perform *Our American Cousin* in Ford's Theatre in Washington, D.C., on April 14, 1865. It was almost exactly five years later on April 19, 1870, Augustans saw Keene perform the same role in *Our American Cousin* in Girardey's Opera House in the 800 block of Broad Street. (Courtesy *The Augusta Chronicle.*)

(below, left and right) EDWIN BOOTH AND ADVERTISEMENT. The famous tragedian Edwin Booth, shown here in his famous lead role, Hamlet, performed the play *Hamlet* in Augusta's Concert Hall on February 10, 1858. He repeated the role in the Opera House on January 28, 1876, just 11 years after his brother, John Wilkes Booth, shot and killed President Abraham Lincoln. The father of the Booth brothers, Junius Brutus Booth, also performed *Hamlet* in Augusta's Theater on April 4, 1822, and the third brother, Junius Brutus Booth Jr., performed the same play with his wife in Girardey's Opera House on April 20, 1872. (Courtesy *The Augusta Chronicle.*)

New Advertisements

Opera House.

BOOTH.

Mr. JOHN T. FORD..............Manager.

Bid the players make haste —HAMLET.

The Eminent Shakspearian Actor,

Mr. Edwin Booth,

Aided by the Popular Young Tragedian,

MR. FREDERICK B. WARD,

Of Booth's Theatre, New York,

And a Specially Selected Dramatic Company.

FRIDAY, Jan. 28, HAMLET.

SATURDAY, Jan. 29, RICHELIEU.

Secured Places, $2 each. The sale of Tickets will commence on Saturday, January 22, at the Music store of Geo. A. Oates & Son.
jan16-2w

WASHINGTON'S BIRTHDAY. Patriotic celebrations always have been a form of entertainment in the Augusta area. Here, from left to right, Eleanor Rucker, Mary May Wells, Elizabeth Ricker, Clara Nell Fortune, and Rickman Ferris take part in the celebration of President George Washington's birthday on February 27, 1927, at Meadow Garden, former home of Declaration of Independence signer George Walton. The celebration was organized by the Augusta Chapter of the Daughters of the American Revolution. (Courtesy Harry Vaiden.)

SARAH BERNHARDT. This great French actress was on her farewell tour of America and 72 years old with a leg amputated when she performed scenes from four plays, including *The Death of Cleopatra* and *Camille* on January 11, 1917, in the Grand Opera House at Greene and Eighth Streets. The review the next day noted, "There has been only one Sarah Bernhardt. There will never be another like her, and Augusta looked upon her for doubtless the last time last night." Reportedly, 250,000 turned out for the funeral of the "Divine Sarah" in Paris in 1923. (Advertisement courtesy *The Augusta Chronicle*.)

CHARLIE CHAPLIN. The legendary English-born comedian came to Augusta on his 29th birthday, April 16, 1918, to promote the sale of Liberty Bonds. Chaplin and his party arrived by train from Columbia, South Carolina, at 1:45 p.m. and went to the Albion Hotel in the 700 block of Broad Street to freshen up. They then walked across the street to the newly-opened Wells Theater (later renamed The Imperial) and spoke to an overflow crowd at 2:30 p.m. They next were driven to the Camp Hancock hospital, where Chaplin distributed cigarettes throughout the wards. He was given a birthday dinner at 5:30 p.m. (hosted by Judge Henry Hammond) at the Augusta Country Club and at 9:15 p.m. boarded a train for Macon. (Courtesy HBO Cable TV Network.)

ALBION HOTEL. The hotel where Charlie Chaplin stayed in 1918 was also where Ty Cobb stayed in 1904 and 1905 when he was an Augusta Tourist baseball player. And it was where Cobb on November 18, 1911, met New Jersey governor Woodrow Wilson at an afternoon reception. That night Governor Wilson, who spent his childhood in Augusta, saw Cobb perform in the play *The College Widow* around the corner from the Albion at the Grand Opera House. Cobb played not a baseball player but a football hero. (Courtesy Joseph Lee III.)

CONCERT HALL!

AN INSTRUMENTAL

CONCERT,

WILL BE GIVEN BY

MR. HETT AND HIS PUPILS,

ASSISTED BY PROF. HILLENS,

Wednesday Eve'g,

APRIL 4th,

At Concert Hall.

PROGRAMME.

PART I.

1. Potpourri, Norma, 4 Violins and Piano,
   Performed by J. Bignon, T. Dortic, G. Goodrich & A. Brandt.
2. Belisario, Fantasia for Violin and Piano, - Theo. Dortic.
3. Dreams on the Ocean, Violin and Piano, - J. Bignon.
4. Crystal Palace Polka, Flute and Violin, - C. Bignon & P. Simmons.
5. Rays of Hope, Waltz, Violin and Piano, - Geo. Goodrich.
6. Anvil Chorus, T. Dortic, J. Bignon, G. Goodrich, A. Brandt, T. Clark, and Platt.

CONCERT HALL. This was an early program for the Concert Hall, which was a major place for local entertainment in the mid-1800s. It was located on the south side of the 800 block of Broad Street with its entrance on Ellis Street. Isador P. Girardy, who became its "sole proprietor" in May of 1869, remodeled the building and reopened it on November 22, 1869, as Girardy's Opera House. English playwright Oscar Wilde spoke in Girardy's, by then renamed Augusta Opera House, on July 6, 1882. William F. "Buffalo Bill" Cody appeared here on October 8, 1878. The building burned on April 1, 1883, coincidentally just seven months after the opening of the New Masonic Theatre in the next block. (Courtesy the Augusta Museum of History.)

THOMAS GREENE BETHUNE. This child piano prodigy was born on May 25, 1849, near Columbus, Georgia, in Harris County, as Thomas Greene Wiggins. He and his parents were sold to Gen. James Neil Bethune shortly after his birth, and he assumed Bethune as his last name. The Bethune family, all musicians, encouraged Tom's musical development. Tom presented his first public piano performance in Columbus on October 7, 1857, and appeared in Augusta's Masonic Hall for the first time a few months later on February 23 and 24 of 1858. He was only nine years old. This advertisement is for his appearances on November 13 and 15, 1861. (Courtesy *The Augusta Chronicle and Sentinel*.)

MASONIC HALL.

TOM,

The Blind Negro Boy

PIANIST,

THE

WONDER OF THE WORLD,

THE MARVEL OF THE AGE!

This mysterious child will give two of his inimitable Entertainments in this city, on

Wednesday and Friday Evenings,

13TH AND 15TH INSTS.,

AT MASONIC HALL,

FOR THE BENEFIT OF OUR'

Sick and Wounded Soldiers!

Doors open at 6½; Concert to commence at 7¾ o'clock P. M
Admission 50 cents; Children and servants 25 cents.
For particulars see small bills.   nov13

GRAND PRESENTS ROSE STAHL. Actress Rose Stahl was presented in the Grand Opera House at Greene and Eighth Streets by Charles Frohman on January 10, 1917, to perform in *Our Mrs. McChesney*. She was described in the *Chronicle* as having "versatility" and a "delicious sense of humor." The newspaper article observed, "When the McChesney stories were written by Edna Ferber [later to write *Show Boat*, *Giant*, and other novels], she had Miss Stahl in mind, having been greatly attracted by Miss Stahl's wonderful portrayal of 'The Chorus Lady' and 'Maggie Pepper.' " (Courtesy the Augusta Museum of History.)

Grand Opera House
AUGUSTA, GEORGIA
Season 1916-1917

WEDNESDAY, JANUARY 10, 1917
CHARLES FROHMAN Presents

ROSE STAHL
IN A NEW AMERICAN COMEDY

Our Mrs. McChesney
(A Dramatization of Edna Ferber's McChesney Stories)
By George V. Hobart and Edna Ferber
BY ARRANGEMENT WITH JOSEPH BROOKS

THE CHARACTERS:
(In the order in which they speak)
Harry Slight, Clerk of the Sloane House............John Will
Minnie, the cigar girl............May Wood

SEÑOR ANDONEGUI. This Hispanic violinist came to Augusta for a concert in May of 1902 and apparently stayed. He was in the city only a few months when he presented the Andonegui Orchestra for the first time in Miller-Walker Hall on November 10, 1902. The orchestra was composed of 26 talented local citizens. He married Augustan Helen Taylor about 1917 and they had a son and a daughter. Andonegui presented a series of free concerts on Sundays in the Grand Opera House in 1916 and 1917 that educated many young and poor Augustans about classical music. He and his family moved from Augusta in September 1920 to Richmond, Virginia. He died February 15, 1941, in Mexico City, where he had gone to improve his health, and was buried there. His son, Lt. Jose Andonegui, was killed in World War II that same year. His widow, Helen, died in January 1970 and was buried in Laurens, South Carolina. (Courtesy the Augusta Museum of History.)

LILLIAN RUSSELL. The actress and ballad singer (born Helen Louise Leonard in Clinton, Iowa) was regarded as the ideal of feminine beauty in the last part of the 19th century, known as the Gay Nineties. She performed several times in Augusta, including January 11, 1910, in *The First Night* and January 7, 1914, in a vaudeville revue that included western silent movie star William Farnum. Both performances were in the Grand Opera House on Greene Street. (Courtesy *The Augusta Chronicle*.)

GEN. TOM THUMB. Show impresario P.T. Barnum's tiny discovery, Tom Thumb (actually Connecticut-born Charles Sherwood Stratton) came to Augusta repeatedly (1843, 1848, 1868, 1876), including these appearances on Christmas Eve and Christmas Day of 1868 in the Concert Hall on Broad Street. He brought with him three other small folks, including his wife, Lavinia Warren Stratton, whom he had married five years earlier. Tom Thumb, at his first Augusta appearance in April 1843, was said to be 11 years old, stand 25 inches high, and weigh only 15 pounds. The truth is he was just five years old but still was very small for his age. (Courtesy *The Augusta Chronicle and Sentinel*.)

POSITIVELY, TWO DAYS ONLY !

AT CONCERT HALL,

THURSDAY AND · FRIDAY, DEC. 24TH AND 25TH.

THURSDAY ONE LEVEE AT 7½ P. M., Friday (Christmas Day) three levees, at 11 A. M., 3 and 7½ P. M. *1868*

GEN. TOM. THUMB
AND HIS LITTLE PARTY.

Gen. Tom Thumb's party, consisting of the Original and World-renowned GEN. TOM THUMB and his beautiful and accomplished little Wife, Mrs. LAVINIA WARREN STRATTON; that Inimitable Specimen of Wit, Skill, Agility and Comic Drollery, COMMODORE NUTT (known as "$30,000 Nutt), and his intended wife, the sweet little Sprite, MISS Ↄ INNIE WARREN.

Ladies and Children are considerately advised to attend the *day* exhibition, and thus avoid the crowd and confusion of the evening performance.

Admission 25 cents. Children under ten years of age 15 cents. Reserved Seats, 50 cents. Children under ten years, 25 cents.

dec22—4   NED DAVIS, Agent.

16

BUFFALO BILL CODY, ADVERTISEMENT FROM 1895. Many pioneer Augustans headed for the Wild West, but the Wild West came to Augusta in the late 19th century and early 20th century through the showmanship of Buffalo Bill Cody. His documented appearances include October 8–9, 1878, in the Augusta Opera House (exhibiting the scalp of Indian Chief Yellow Hand, whom he claimed to have killed in battle two years earlier); October 18, 1895, in a covered grandstand (accompanied by sharpshooter Annie Oakley); October 23, 1901 (with more than 600 performers that also included Miss Oakley); and October 28, 1912, his last appearance. (Courtesy *The Augusta Chronicle*.)

RIVERWALK DEDICATION. This large crowd turned out on April Fool's Day of 1988 on Eighth Street at the Levee for the official dedication of Riverwalk. Sitting third to the left of the man with the Colonial hat is Augusta mayor Charles A. DeVaney. This area of Riverwalk now boasts a beautiful fountain and has been used countless times by local arts groups. (Photo by Jeff Barnes; Courtesy *The Augusta Chronicle*.)

JESSYE NORMAN AMPHITHEATER. The grand opening of the Riverwalk Amphitheater, Ninth Street at the Levee, on June 15, 1990, was a major boost to Augusta's entertainment scene. The opening acts were a trio of guys called The Lettermen, shown here taking the stage, and a quartet of ladies called Eclipse. The amphitheater later would be used for such diverse events as concerts, free movies, Easter Sunrise services, and a political rally for presidential candidate Bill Clinton. It also would be renamed for Augusta native and opera superstar Jessye Norman. (Photo by Eric Olig; Courtesy *The Augusta Chronicle*.)

18

Two

THE GROWTH OF
AREA ARTS

As Augusta grew in the 19th and 20th centuries, so did its arts organizations. Groups cheering up Augustans during the Civil War included the Ladies Volunteer Association, the Houghton Club, the Philharmonic Society, and the Augusta Choral Society.

Acting and performing groups in the late 19th and early 20th centuries included the Montrose Dramatic Club with plays in Summerville Academy, the Paint and Powder Club with plays in the Grand Opera House, and the Little Theatre League, who bought a former Lutheran Church on Walker Street in 1931 and turned it into a 310-seat theater.

Musical groups also began blossoming including the Clef Club, an organization of black singers and musicians that presented classical concerts in Trinity C.M.E. Church as early as 1922.

MORRIS MUSEUM OF ART. Among the early visitors to the Morris Museum of Art at 10th and Reynolds Streets was George Allen of Evans, Georgia, who gave his son, James, an eye-level view of the paintings. Augusta's cultural scene took a giant step forward when the 18,000-square-foot Morris Museum of Art officially opened September 24, 1992. Its large collection focuses on art either by Southern-born artists or with a Southern theme. The museum was created by Augusta native William S. Morris III in honor of his parents, Florence and William S. Morris Jr. (Photo by Blake Madden; Courtesy *The Augusta Chronicle*.)

19

RUBY LORRAINE RADFORD. This noted Augustan in January of 1928 co-founded the Augusta Authors Club, currently Augusta's oldest arts organization, with Constance Lewis and Dr. Lawton Evans. She became the group's first secretary, with Dr. Evans as its first president. Her literary output included more than 50 books and several hundred short stories, magazine serials, and plays. Shown here at a tea on May 25, 1961, are, from left to right, LePage Bailey, Ruby Lorraine Radford, and Mrs. Henry Gilbert. The book by Radford that they are viewing, *Once Upon A Spring*, was dedicated to Bailey and her husband, Dr. Joseph P. Bailey Jr. (Breault Newsfoto; Courtesy *The Augusta Chronicle*.)

LAWTON B. EVANS. The first Augusta Authors Club president wrote a series of books for young people and textbooks on Georgia history used by both grade school and high school students until 1938. He himself graduated at 17 from Emory College in 1880 as valedictorian of his class. He earned his master's degree at the University of Georgia and began teaching eighth grade in Augusta. He was elected Richmond County school superintendent in November 1882 and held that position until his death on April 6, 1934. He guided the consolidation of all Richmond County schools into a single system. (Courtesy *The Augusta Chronicle*.)

MISS AMERICA IN TOWN. Oklahoma native Susan Powell, Miss America 1981, was in Augusta in 1989 with her actor/vocalist husband David Parsons. She was Laurey and he was Curly in The Augusta Opera's production of *Oklahoma!*, presented in the Imperial Theater on September 10–12 and 14–16. The Augusta Opera was formed in 1967 by two Fort Gordon soldiers, Ian Strasfogel and James Brooks Jr. They formed a local opera association and "engaged" Harry Jacobs as musical director. The first production of the opera company was Giacomo Puccini's *La Boheme* in Bell Auditorium's Music Hall on September 15, 1967. (Photo by Steve Thackston; Courtesy *The Augusta Chronicle*.)

AUGUSTA COLLEGE OPERA. Many William Gilbert and Arthur Sullivan operas were presented at Augusta College (later Augusta State) under the leadership of William "Bill" Toole, then director of the college's fine arts department. This opera, *The Mikado*, produced by Toole and stage directed by Ray Menard, was performed April 26–28, 1985, in the Grover C. Maxwell Performing Arts Theater on campus in commemoration of the 100th anniversary of the first performance of *The Mikado*. (Photo by Shaun Stanley; Courtesy *The Augusta Chronicle*.)

TUESDAY'S MUSIC LIVE. Some of the most popular entertainment diversions in downtown have been the free Tuesday's Music Live series of concerts at noon in St. Paul's Episcopal Church, on Sixth at Reynolds, started by Augusta first lady Gwen Fulcher Young and St. Paul's music director Keith Shafer. Here the Troika Balalaikas trio from Atlanta—from left to right, Lynn McConnell, Dave Cooper, and Gregory Corageorge—perform Russian folk songs on February 11, 1992. (Photo by Rudy Nyhoff; Courtesy *The Augusta Chronicle*.)

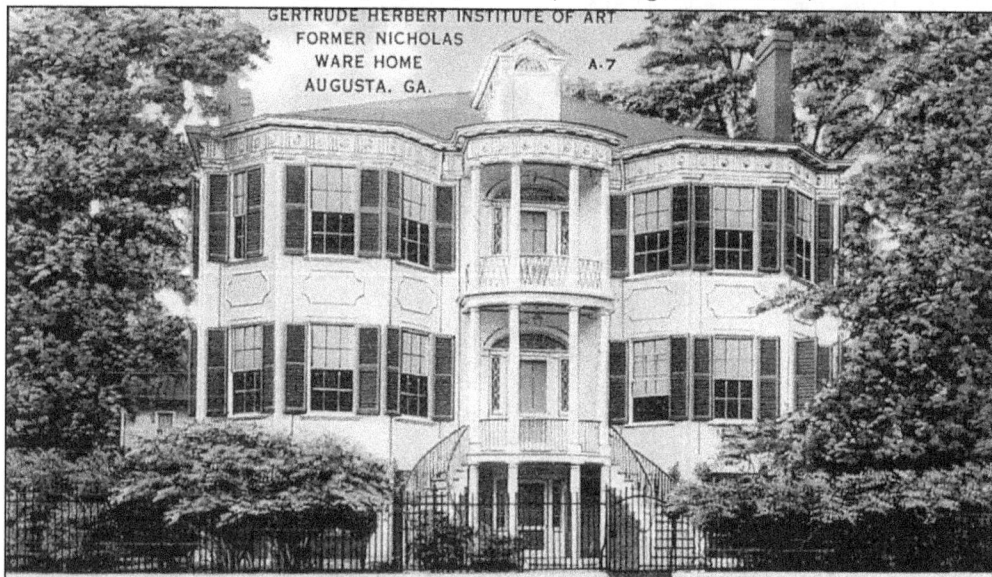

GERTRUDE HERBERT INSTITUTE OF ART. Professional and amateur painters have been entertaining Augustans with their creations since the 1700s. Many have utilized this building constructed in 1818 by Nicholas Ware, the year before he became mayor of Augusta. The home at 506 Telfair Street became an art center in 1937 when Olivia Antoinette Herbert bought it and established an art endowment in memory of her late daughter, Gertrude Herbert Dunn. (Postcard courtesy author's collection.)

22

AUGUSTA MUSEUM OF HISTORY. Steam engine 302, said to be the last surviving steam locomotive of the Georgia Railroad, was moved on September 8, 1993, to its new home at the Augusta Museum of History (then the Augusta-Richmond County Museum) at Sixth and Reynolds Streets. The engine previously was on display for several years at the old Augusta-Richmond County Museum on Telfair Street and for many years before that at Pendleton King Park. (Photo by Blake Madden; Courtesy *The Augusta Chronicle*.)

HEARTH OF EMBERS. Contemporary as well as classical productions have been the hallmark of The Augusta Ballet. The company is shown here rehearsing *Hearth of Embers*, which it performed October 6–8, 1989, in the Imperial Theater. The dancers, from left to right, are Peter Powlus, Cammy Fisher, Ken Busbin, and Renee Toole. (Photo by Steve Thackston; Courtesy *The Augusta Chronicle*.)

SALLIE CARLSON. The Augusta Civic Ballet was formed in June of 1962 with its first director and chief choreographer Sallie Chadwick Carlson, a native of Detroit, Michigan. She moved to Augusta at the age of 12 with her parents, who became Augusta dance instructors. The Civic Ballet's debut performance was *Allegresse*, set to Sergei Prokofiev's *Classical Symphony*, on December 21, 1962, in the Music Hall section of Bell Auditorium. The Augusta Symphony, led by Harry Jacobs, provided the music. The Civic Ballet was reincorporated in 1968 as the Augusta Ballet. (Courtesy *The Augusta Chronicle*.)

AUGUSTA CHORAL
SOCIETY. Emily Remington
was the founder of the
modern version of the
Augusta Choral Society in
1951. Its debut, George
Frederick Handel's *Messiah*,
came December 9, 1951, in
Post Theater No. 3 at then
Camp Gordon. Shown here,
from left to right, are Jessye
Norman (opera singer and
Remington's former voice
student), Remington, and
Mrs. John Adamson going
over music. The Choral
Society and Augusta
Symphony co-sponsored a
performance by Norman,
accompanied by pianist
Remington, in the Music
Hall section of Bell
Auditorium on February 1,
1970. (Courtesy *The
Augusta Chronicle*.)

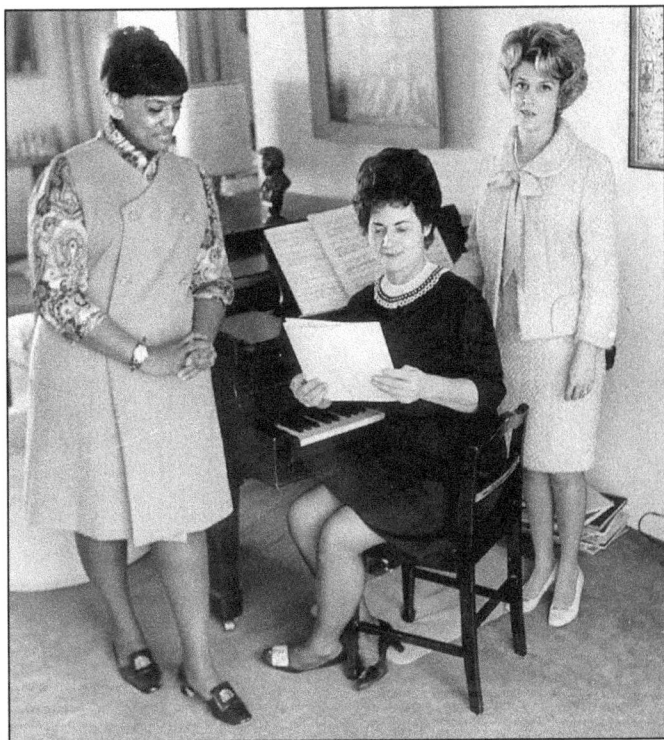

SINGING IN HOLY TRINITY. Eloy
Fominaya directs the Augusta Choral
Society in a rehearsal for the group's
March 28, 1987 spring concert at the
Church of the Most Holy Trinity. The
performance featured 80 voices and a 14-
piece chamber orchestra. (Photo by Rudy
Nyhoff; Courtesy *The Augusta Chronicle*.)

JOHN PHILIP SOUSA. The "March King" was a favorite of Augustans for several decades. He made at least eight appearances in the city: April 22, 1895; January 27, 1899; February 8, 1902; February 3, 1906; January 21, 1908; February 21, 1924; February 25, 1926; and November 7, 1930. He appeared in the Augusta Opera House and the Imperial Theater and made his last appearances at 3:15 and 8:30 p.m. in the Academy of Richmond County school auditorium on November 7, 1930. He was 76. Mayor William B. Bell proclaimed that occasion "Sousa Day" in the city. The conductor died two years later. (Drawing published in the *Augusta Herald*.)

EVENINGS IN APPLEBY GARDEN. Usually the summer concerts organized by the Augusta-Richmond County Regional Library are presented outdoors behind the Appleby library branch at Johns Road and Walton Way. But this concert of pianists Allen Baston and Charlotte Wilkie on June 16, 1991, opening the series' 37th season, was forced inside due to rain. The overflow audience watched through the doorway. The first Appleby outdoor event on June 14, 1955, offered recorded music and a short musical film. (Photo by Mark Dolejs; Courtesy *The Augusta Chronicle*.)

GEORGIA RAILROAD CONCERT BAND. This band sponsored by the Georgia Railroad bank was directed by Louis Sayre. He also was organist at St. Paul's Episcopal Church and organist at the Imperial Theater. Sayre wrote many localized compositions, including the "Greater Augusta March" and the "Camp Hancock March," which was even played by John Philip Sousa's band. The Georgia Railroad Concert Band, shown here about 1926, included female bass drummer Hazel Wilson. (Courtesy Travis Barnes.)

AUGUSTA CONCERT BAND. Alan Drake, founding director of this large group of community musicians, conducts the band in one of its many concerts. He was a professor of music at Augusta College for many years before retiring and also was the principal clarinet player in the Augusta Symphony between 1982 and 1989. Among the many concerts of the Augusta Concert Band have been the annual Empty Stocking Fund Christmas concerts and the outdoor performances in Riverwalk Amphitheater. (Photo by Robert Seale; Courtesy *The Augusta Chronicle*.)

27

MUNICIPAL AUDITORIUM. The city auditorium, which cost $440,000, was dedicated on March 31, 1940, with 3,560 seats in the main section and 929 in the rear Music Hall section. Both sections used the same stage. It originally was called Municipal Auditorium but was renamed the William B. Bell Auditorium in 1951 in honor of the progressive Augusta mayor. Its first booking event was the two-day, fourth annual Augusta Fat Cattle Show and Sale. (Courtesy *The Augusta Chronicle.*)

RAINING IN THE BELL. This memorable photo of Bell patrons on January 6, 1977, using umbrellas during a Glenn Miller Orchestra concert illustrated the need for repairs to the Bell. The auditorium was closed in November of 1982, mainly due to fire hazards, and reopened October 11, 1990, after extensive remodeling. The renovation included the demolition of the Music Hall section to create a loading dock and the reduction of about 1,000 seats in the main section. (Photo by Rickey Pittman; Courtesy *The Augusta Chronicle.*)

THE AUGUSTA PLAYERS. This long-running acting group, formed in early September 1945 with meetings at the Academy of Richmond County, was spearheaded by Louisa Mustin. She became chairman of the first play reading committee and offered to underwrite expenses of the first production. The Augusta Players' first offering, *Kind Lady*, was presented in the Music Hall section of Bell Auditorium on November 15–16, 1945. Here is a scene from *The Mouse That Roared*, performed December 12–14, 1963, in the Players' playhouse on Lake Forest Drive. The actors are, from left to right, (front row) John Lake and Bob Watkins; (back row) Jack Seigler and Julian Stewart. (Photo by Robert Symms; Courtesy Fitz-Symms Studio.)

LOUISA MUSTIN. Before her death in 1976, Louisa Mustin was a mover and shaker on Augusta's arts scene. She not only founded the Augusta Players in 1945, but she also founded Planned Parenthood of Augusta and was a founding member of the Augusta Art Club in 1932. She also was past president of the Junior League and was active in the League of Women Voters. She personally built the first permanent theater in America in 1950 exclusively for the presentation of puppet plays, which lasted four years at 1469 Broad Street. About 100 of her unique puppet creations, known as "doll actors," are in the archives of the theater department at the University of North Carolina at Chapel-Hill. (Courtesy Sam Singal.)

STORYLAND THEATRE. The debut production of the independent Storyland Theatre was *Beware What You Ask Of A Fairy*, presented November 30 to December 2 in the Maxwell Theater at Augusta College. The original play, authored by Rick Davis, featured, from left to right, Saundra Clements, Chantey Bruni, Jennifer Dushku, Matt Stovall, Peggy Williams, Barbara Lynne Feldman, and Jeff Pullium. The group of adult actors doing children's plays was founded by Feldman, who is still president and executive director. The group has given back more than $100,000 to the community including acting scholarships. (Photo by Bill Johnson; Courtesy Storyland Theatre.)

GIANT PUPPETS IN TOWN. These nine-foot-tall puppets from the Bits 'N Pieces Puppet Theater in Tampa, Florida, were seen at the 1986 and 1987 Arts in the Heart of Augusta arts festivals held in the Municipal Building's parking lot. The group performed *Rip Van Winkle* in 1986 and *The Ugly Duckling* in 1987. The Greater Augusta Arts Council, which sponsors the festivals, met for the first time on February 19, 1968, in Aldersgate Methodist Church, with Clarence R. Jones selected as the first chairman. (Photo by Don Rhodes.)

FORT GORDON DINNER THEATRE. After 15 years in an old wooden building, the Fort Gordon Dinner Theatre moved into a remodeled post movie theater and opened with the musical *Big River: The Adventures of Huckleberry Finn* on August 16, 1991. Here, Huck Finn (played by Greg Goodwin, currently general manager of the Imperial Theater) is being pushed out of his chair by rowdy cast members. (Photo by Margaret Sellers; Courtesy *The Augusta Chronicle*.)

AUGUSTA MINI THEATER. Tyrone Butler and his wife, Judith, right, in January of 1986 helped Michelle Rouse recite a poem as the Augusta Mini Theatre's contribution to the city of Augusta's 250th birthday party. Mr. Butler founded the Mini Theatre under the sponsorship of the Opportunities Industrialization Center. The group presented its first effort on October 8, 1975, in the Wallace library branch followed by a Christmas show on December 17 at Lucy C. Laney High School. (Photo by Judy Ondrey; Courtesy *The Augusta Chronicle*.)

LINDA AND ED BRADBERRY. This dynamic and creative couple met in 1961 at the University of Georgia where both were studying piano. They married in Augusta in 1962 and began teaching piano to scores of Augustans. Mr. Bradberry played with the Newport Jazz Quintet and the Boston University Symphony while a student at Boston University. He later became general director of the Augusta Opera. Mrs. Bradberry would direct more than 50 voices of the Augusta Children's Chorale. (Breault Newsfoto by Jim King; Courtesy *The Augusta Chronicle.*)

RON COLTON. The Augusta Civic Ballet was created by Sallie Carlson but blossomed under the creative choreography of Ron Colton. The Chicagoan was hired in 1964 as artistic director. Carlson later said, "We came up with the idea for the Augusta Civic Ballet and took it so far, but it was Ron Colton who really made the company what it has become." Here he reviews choreography of a show with, from left to right, Laura Laircey, Dale Thompson, Kathy Keith, and Ashley Ledford. (Photo by Phillip Powell; Courtesy *The Augusta Chronicle.*)

HARRY JACOBS. This rehearsal of The Augusta Symphony in September 1988 shows, from left to right, Sarah Paul, Robert Leibholz, Clay Purdy, conductor Harry Jacobs, Alan Drake, Julianne Johnston, and Valerie DiCarlo. The Augusta Symphony began in early 1954 with 15 members as the Augusta Civic Orchestra. Its debut was May 23, 1954, in the Music Hall of Bell Auditorium with Jacobs as director and Sophie Wolski as guest soloist. Jacobs led the symphony for 37 years until retiring in 1991. (Photo by Rudy Nyhoff, Courtesy *The Augusta Chronicle*.)

DONALD PORTNOY. The Augusta Symphony was taken to greater heights with the hiring of Donald Portnoy in 1991 as conductor and music director. He made his debut as conductor on October 5, 1991, opening the Symphony's 37th season. He also created the Augusta Symphony Chamber Orchestra, which had its debut November 24, 1991, in Trinity-On-The-Hill United Methodist Church. Portnoy, also a string musician, is shown here as music director designate on December 12, 1990. He previously founded the University of South Carolina Chamber Orchestra. (Photo by Blake Madden; Courtesy *The Augusta Chronicle*.)

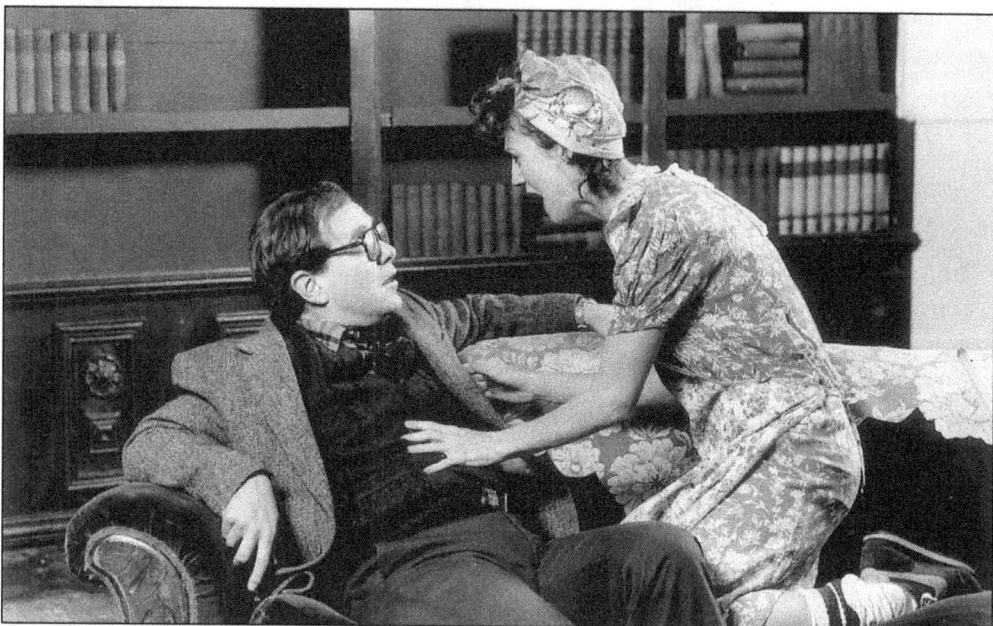

ELIZABETH AND STEVE WALPERT. One of Augusta's best-known married entertainment couples has been Betty and Steve Walpert, shown here on January 5, 1990, rehearsing a scene from *The Housekeeper* for the Fort Gordon Dinner Theatre. Steve has been director of the Fort Gordon Music and Theater Program. Betty (Elizabeth Nelson-Walpert) has served as director of Fort Gordon's Unit Entertainment Program and drama instructor at Davidson Fine Arts Magnet School. (Photo by Margaret Moore; Courtesy *The Augusta Chronicle*.)

JIM AND MATT STOVALL. Two of Augusta's legendary amateur actors and directors were Jim Stovall and his son, Matt, who both also possessed excellent dramatic singing voices. Jim, at left, rehearses a play here with his son at the Stovall family home on January 10, 1984. Jim and Matt both directed many shows for area community and school groups, and Matt became a well-known local radio personality. Jim died on July 4, 1989, and Matt died November 20, 2002. (Photo by Judy Ondrey; Courtesy *The Augusta Chronicle*.)

J.C. Taylor. Theatrical offerings at Paine College were made even more special through the leadership of J.C. Taylor, who directed many performances in the Odeum classroom of Gilbert-Lambuth Memorial Chapel. Shown here on February 19, 1991, rehearsing a one-act comedy of stories are, from left to right, director Taylor, Sharon Parker, Jacqulyne Ephran, Natasha Watkins, and Leslie Stokes. (Photo by Eric Olig, Courtesy *The Augusta Chronicle*.)

Duncan Smith. Many of Augusta College's dramatic productions and musicals were directed by Duncan Smith. Shown here, from left to right, on February 23, 1985, in a scene from the British comedy *Living Together*, are Dee Dunbar, Debbie Ciceri, David Bartlett, Smith, and Donnie Herne. (Photo by Judy Ondrey; Courtesy *The Augusta Chronicle*.)

THEATERS ON BROAD. This expansive photograph taken in late August of 1947 shows the Imperial (showing *Beast With Five Fingers*) and Rialto (*Six Gun Serenade*) theaters in the 700 block of Broad Street and the Modjeska (*Wild Country*) in the 800 block. The Modjeska and Imperial are in use today as show places, while the Rialto is now used by optometrist Dr. Thomas V. Casella, who appreciates the building's unique history. (Photo by Morgan Fitz; Courtesy Fitz-Symms Studio.)

Three

STAGES AND SCREENS

Two significant cultural developments in Augusta in the late 1800s were electric lights (1884), which replaced gas lights in theaters and improved nighttime theatrical offerings, as well as the miracle of motion pictures.

Thomas Edison's Kenetoscope, showing moving pictures in Augusta on January 20, 1895, elicited an article in The Augusta Chronicle noting, "It is all too wonderful to grasp in a moment or in an hour and too wondrous to attempt to describe."

The Star Theater, 723 Broad Street, by 1904 was showing both "Edison's Biograph Moving Pictures" two shows a night (general admission 10¢) and combining it with vaudeville performers.

Meanwhile several silent movies actually were being made totally or partially in Augusta, including The Littlest Rebel in 1914, From The Valley of the Missing in 1915, The New Governor in 1915, Charity in 1916 (co-starring Mrs. D.W. Griffith), The Great Moment in 1918, and The Arizona Bandit filmed in North Augusta in 1920.

MILTON BERLE. Once a performer in Augusta during its vaudeville period, television legend Milton Berle returned to the city on November 12, 1992. The 84-year-old actor returned as a special advisor to the President's Council on Physical Fitness and Sports. He is shown talking at the Brandon Wilde Retirement Center on Washington Road with James Ellis, also 84, laughing at Berle's jokes. (Photo by Margaret Moore Sellers; Courtesy *The Augusta Chronicle*.)

STRAND THEATER. The Strand movie theater was located in the Harrison Building on the south side of the 700 block of Broad Street near Eighth. This photo shows *The Stolen Kiss*, with Constance Binney, being offered there. Since it was filmed in 1920, that movie had to be showing shortly before the Harrison Building burned in November of 1921. The Strand is where *The Littlest Rebel*, partly filmed in Augusta, was shown May 25–27, 1915. The Strand, Modjeska, and New Modjeska were sold to Lynch Entertainment on November 14, 1919, which then sold them and three others to Famous Players, Lasky Corp., on January 29, 1920. (Courtesy Reese Library Collection, Augusta State University.)

GRAND OPERA HOUSE. The grand place to go in Augusta in the late 19th century and early 20th century was the Grand Opera House at Eighth and Greene Streets. It later was shortened to just "The Grand." This is where some of Augusta's earliest silent moving pictures were shown and where some of the nation's brightest stars, such as George M. Cohan, appeared. The Grand opened September 19, 1888, with minstrel George Wilson. It burned March 18, 1922, killing manager James Tant, who was also managing the Imperial, and his wife, Lula. The fire was set by an arsonist who never was caught. (Courtesy *The Augusta Chronicle*.)

LEO CARRILLO. The Los Angeles-born actor Leo Carrillo, later famous as Poncho, the partner of TV western hero The Cisco Kid (1950–1956), performed in the Imperial Theater in the play *Lombardi Ltd.* on November 28, 1921, and then returned shortly afterward to repeat the role on February 14, 1922. (Courtesy author's collection.)

AUGUSTA'S THEATER BEAUTIFUL

| FIRST SHOW 7:30 P. M. | **THE WELLS** | SECOND SHOW 9:15 P. M. |

GRAND QPENING TONIGHT

——Presenting——

B. F. KEITH'S SUPREME VAUDEVILLE·

Supplemented by Photoplay Program.

—PRICES—

Matinee 10c, 20c

—EVENING—

NO MATINEE TODAY	Loges 50c	**RESERVED SEATS**
But Daily Perform-ance at 3 O'clock after Today.	Orchestra 35c	These May Be Ob-tained for First Evening Show only. Wiil Hold Seats till 8:15 P. M.
	Balcony—	
	First section 35c	
	Remainder 25c	
	Gallery 15c	

(Plus War Tax)

THE WELLS. The theater Augustans now know as the Imperial opened as the Wells on February 18, 1918, built by Jake Wells of Richmond, Virginia. Its first manager was Richard B. Tant, whose parents died in the Grand Opera House fire in 1922. The Wells closed briefly and then reopened on December 11, 1919, as the Imperial. (Courtesy *The Augusta Chronicle*.)

IMPERIAL REMODELED. Lat Nguyen, left, and Loy Veal of Latco Construction Co. stood on the historic stage of the Imperial on April 10, 1985. They observed their restoration handiwork shortly before the theater reopened on April 17 after being closed almost four years. The renovated Imperial was given a new life and became used for everything from concerts by the Kingston Trio and local rock groups to acting as a rehearsal hall for James Brown's world-wide tours. (Photo by Randy Hill; Courtesy *The Augusta Chronicle*.)

40

CLAUDE CASEY. This former western movie actor and radio personality was in the 1973 movie *Buster & Billie*, filmed around Statesboro, Georgia. Shown are, from left to right, The Sage Dusters, Augusta-area musicians consisting of Charles Reese (steel guitar), Jerry Couch, Tommy Wilson, Claude Casey, Buddy Walker, and Curley Mulliken. Casey recorded for the Decca and MGM labels. He came to Augusta in 1951 to work for radio station WGAC and later became owner, president, and general manager of WJES radio in Johnston, South Carolina. (Courtesy Columbia Pictures.)

INTERIOR VIEW-DREAMLAND THEATRE-AUGUSTA, GA.

DREAMLAND THEATER. The Dreamland Theater on the corner of Broad and Ninth Streets was operating as the Superba in February of 1908. It was enlarged and reopened as the Dreamland on September 27, 1909, boasting 12 large ceiling fans. The building burned February 3, 1945, but wasn't demolished until July of 1948. It was advertising in 1917 "the best in moving pictures, six reels daily." (Courtesy the Augusta Museum of History.)

Modjeska	NEW MODJESKA	STRAND
MONDAY VALESKA SURATT — in — 'The Straight-Way'	PROGRAM **Marcus Loew's** **VAUDEVILLE** Direct from New York to Augusta	MONDAY Wm. S. HART — in — "The Return of Drawegan"
TUESDAY LOUISE LOVELY — in — "Bettina Loved a Soldier"	THURSDAY FRIDAY SATURDAY A "The Bugler of Algiers" A Thrilling Story in Five Acts	TUESDAY FANNIE WARD — in — "The Years of the Locust"
WEDNESDAY ALICE BRADY — in — "Bought and Paid For"	B **Dolly Morrissey** Songland's Sweetest Singers C **Keene & Williams** In Their Rural Comedy "Almost Married"	WEDNESDAY PAULINE FREDERICK — in — "AUDREY"
THURSDAY MARY MILES MINTER — in — "A Dream or Two Ago"	D **Frank Gabbay & Co.** Vaudeville Versatile Ventriloquist E **Neil McKinley**	THURSDAY SIR HERBERT TREE — in — "The Old Folks at Home"
FRIDAY VIOLA DANA — in — "The Cossack Whip"	The Raving Nut Comedian F **JAS. HORAN PRESENTS** "IN THE CAMP" With Billy McDermott & Marty Moray 8 Beauties from the Peach Orchard	FRIDAY MARGUERITE CLARK — in — "Miss George Washington"
SATURDAY CHARLIE CHAPLIN — in — 'Behind the Screen'	MATINEE 3 P. M. Orchestra .... 25c Mezzanine .. 15c	EVENING, 8:30 Orchestra .... 50c Orc. Boxes .. 50c Mezzanine ....25c Mez. Loges 35c	SATURDAY MME. PETROVA — in — "Extravagance"
Prices Always 5c and 10c	Seat Sale Opens Tuesday 10 a. m.	Prices Always 5c and 10c

MODJESKA THEATER. The first Modjeska Theater opened August 3, 1911, on the south side of the 800 block of Broad Street and was named after popular actress and Augusta visitor Helena Modjeska. The New Modjeska, built by Ty Cobb's father-in-law, Roswell O. Lombard, opened on the north side of Broad on November 30, 1916. The New Modjeska featured Bearden's Orchestra, a six-piece group, furnishing the music for every evening showing of the silent films. (Courtesy *The Augusta Chronicle*.)

TWO MODJESKAS. The above advertisement from *The Augusta Chronicle* shows both the old and new Modjeska theaters were operating at the same time. The New Modjeska, in spite of what a metal plaque on the current building says, did not replace the original Modjeska.

LENOX THEATER. This popular black show place of the early 20th century, now an empty lot, opened on November 29, 1920, at Ninth and Gwinnett (now Laney-Walker Boulevard). It was built by four African-American businessmen: physician Dr. George N. Stoney, restaurant owner John P. Waring Sr., and postal service employees John A. Norflett and William H. Wilburn. It was designed by a white architect, G. Lloyd Preacher, and constructed by a black builder, John S. Mitchell of Orangeburg, South Carolina. The manager of the Lenox, Earl Pinkerton, was one of the most respected citizens of Augusta. He was so well regarded that when the city of Augusta decided to hire African-American police officers, Pinkerton was asked to draw up a list of good candidates. The Lenox featured such famous stars as Cab Calloway, Duke Ellington, Ray Charles, Ruth Brown, and Louis Jordan. (Courtesy the Augusta Museum of History.)

DELMAR CASINO. Another important place for black culture in the early 20th century was the Delmar Casino at Ninth and Walton Way, also now an empty lot. The two-story building was managed by John Crim, related by marriage to Earl Pinkerton. Their wives, Odelle and Mary, were sisters. The Delmar presented many big acts, including Earl "Fatha" Hines, Louis Jordan, and Fletcher Henderson (pianist for Bessie Smith and later a member of the Georgia Music Hall of Fame). The first ad in *The Augusta Chronicle* for the Delmar Casino appeared July 10, 1938, and the last was in July of 1957. (Courtesy the Augusta Museum of History.)

SPIRITS OF HARMONY. Georgia state senator Henry Howard, center, led the Spirits of Harmony gospel singing group and was co-host of the *Parade of Quartets* television show, still airing Sunday mornings on WJBF. His son, Karlton, is now host of the program started by host Steve Manderson. The show is nearing its 50th anniversary and is one of the longest-running television programs of any kind. Henry Howard also started an upholstery business and records sales stores. Other Spirits of Harmony members are, from left to right (front row) Harrison Godbee and Roy Jackson; (back row) George Allen, George Leverett, and Charlie Avery. (Courtesy Henry Howard.)

TROOPER TERRY. Kids around the Central Savannah River Area on Saturday mornings from 1961 to 1981 watched the *Trooper Terry Show*, hosted by Terry Sams on WJBF television station. Sams estimates more than 100,000 boys and girls appeared on his show. He is shown here with his Magic Viewing Screen. The first day Sams went to work for WJBF in 1961, he appeared on camera as a Santa Claus helper. (Courtesy WJBF Television.)

TROY DONAHUE. Movie and television star Troy Donahue, then 30, greeted local fans Bonnie Hammer, left, and Cynthia Manly after arriving at Bush Field Airport. The teen idol and star of the movies *Parrish* and *A Summer Place* and the television series *Surfside 6* made an appearance on June 28, 1967, at Daniel Village Theatre to promote his latest movie *Those Fantastic Flying Fools*. He was back in Augusta on February 20, 1998, at age 62, to star at the Imperial Theater in the touring musical *Bye, Bye, Birdie*. He played Harry MacAfee, the protective father of a girl set to receive a kiss from teen idol Conrad Birdie. Donahue died a few years later on September 2, 2001, from heart failure. (Courtesy *The Augusta Chronicle*.)

THREE FACES PREMIERE. One of Broad Street's most glittery nights was the world premiere of the movie *Three Faces of Eve* at the Miller Theater on September 18, 1957. The movie was based on a book of the same title by Augusta psychiatrists Dr. Corbett H. Thigpen and Dr. Hervey M. Cleckley. The real story told of an Edgefield, South Carolina woman (Chris Costner Sizemore) who had multiple personalities. The movie's script was written by Georgian Nunally Johnson and starred Georgian Joanne Woodward, who won the Best Actress Oscar for her role. She could not attend the premiere because she was filming *The Young Lions* with Marlon Brando. (Photo by Morgan Fitz; Courtesy Fitz-Symms Studio.)

AUTHORS AND WIVES. *Three Faces of Eve* authors Dr. Hervey M. Cleckley, left, and Dr. Corbett H. Thigpen, arrive with their wives at the Bon Air Hotel for a dinner honoring them prior to the premiere. All the VIP movie guests were driven from the Bon Air dinner to the Miller in brand-new Edsel automobiles. (Photo by Morgan Fitz; Courtesy Fitz-Symms Studio.)

SPECIAL GUESTS. Miss Georgia Jody Shattuck and Eleanor Carter, mother of *Three Faces* star Joanne Woodward, were among the honored guests at the premiere. Carter was living in Aiken, South Carolina, at the time of the premiere. Her former husband— father of Joanne Woodward—was Wade Woodward Jr., a former resident of Augusta and North Augusta. (Photo by Morgan Fitz; Courtesy Fitz-Symms Studio.)

GORDON SCOTT. Actor Gordon Scott, the 11th movie Tarzan, came to the Miller Theater on June 24, 1959, to promote his latest film, *Tarzan's Greatest Adventure*. Scott, who majored in physical education at the University of Oregon, was discovered in 1953 by a Hollywood agent while working as a lifeguard in Las Vegas. (Courtesy Paramount Pictures.)

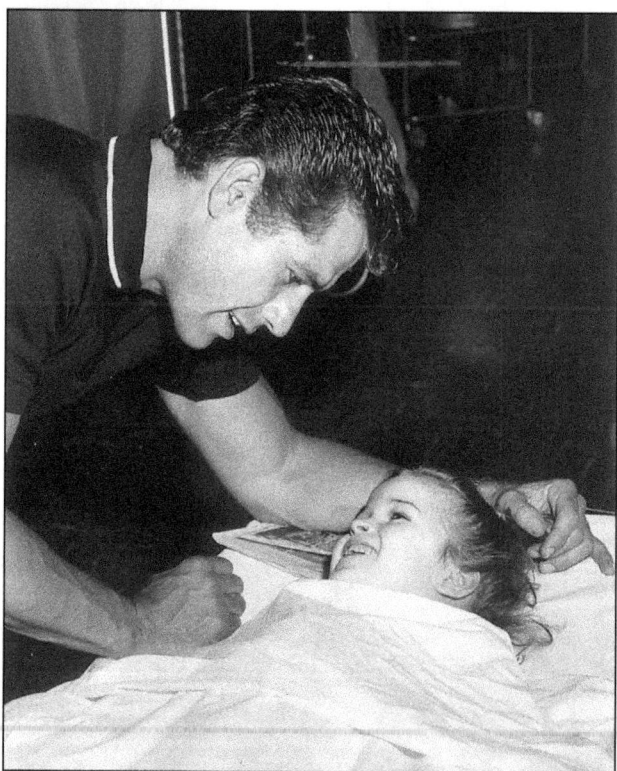

TARZAN VISITS CHILDREN. During his 1959 visit to Augusta, screen Tarzan Gordon Scott visited children in the respiratory ward of Talmadge (now Medical College of Georgia) Hospital. Here he leans over to speak with Gail Morris of Hazelhurst, Georgia. (Photo by and courtesy Robert Symms.)

SUMMER HEAT PREMIERE. Another glittering entertainment evening on Broad Street was the world premiere of *Summer Heat* in the Imperial Theater on May 13, 1987. The movie was based on the novel *Here to Get My Baby Out of Jail* by Augusta resident Louise Shivers, shown here. It co-starred Lori Singer, Anthony Edwards, Bruce Abbott, Kathy Bates, and Clu Gulager. The after-premiere party was held in the park in the middle of Broad in front of the Imperial. Shivers, who sold shoes and records in the Sears store on Walton Way, later became writer-in-residence at Augusta State University. (Photo by Herb Welch; Courtesy *The Augusta Chronicle*.)

WHITTNI WRIGHT. Augustan Whittni Wright was only 6 years old when she co-starred with Nick Nolte and Albert Brooks in the movie *I'll Do Anything*. She is here seen on January 29, 1994, around the time of the movie's release. The next year, she was seen with Jean-Claude Van Damme in *Sudden Death*. (Photo by Rudy Nyhoff; Courtesy *The Augusta Chronicle*.)

GREENE STREET

320 GRAND OPERA HOUSE

GREENE STREET

ELLIS STREET

216 BIJOU

ELLIS STREET

SEVENTH STREET

214 MILLER-WALKER HALL ELITE THEATER

EIGHTH STREET

CONCERT HALL
GIRARDEY'S OPERA HOUSE

| 662 PEERLESS VISITORIUM | 708 MILLER | 740-42 MASONIC TEMPLE NEW MASONIC THEATER | 752-56 HARRISON BLDG. BONITA ARCADIUM THE STRAND | 800-10 MODJESKA | 826-28 AUGUSTA OPERA HOUSE LAFAYETTE HALL ORPHEUM | 838 PEOPLE'S |

BROAD STREET

BROAD STREET

| 641 AUGUSTA FAMILY THEATER | 723 THE STAR | 745 THE WELLS THE IMPERIAL | 767 THE RIALTO | 813-15 NEW MODJESKA | 857 LITTLE GRAND | 879 THEATORIUM SUPERBA DREAMLAND |

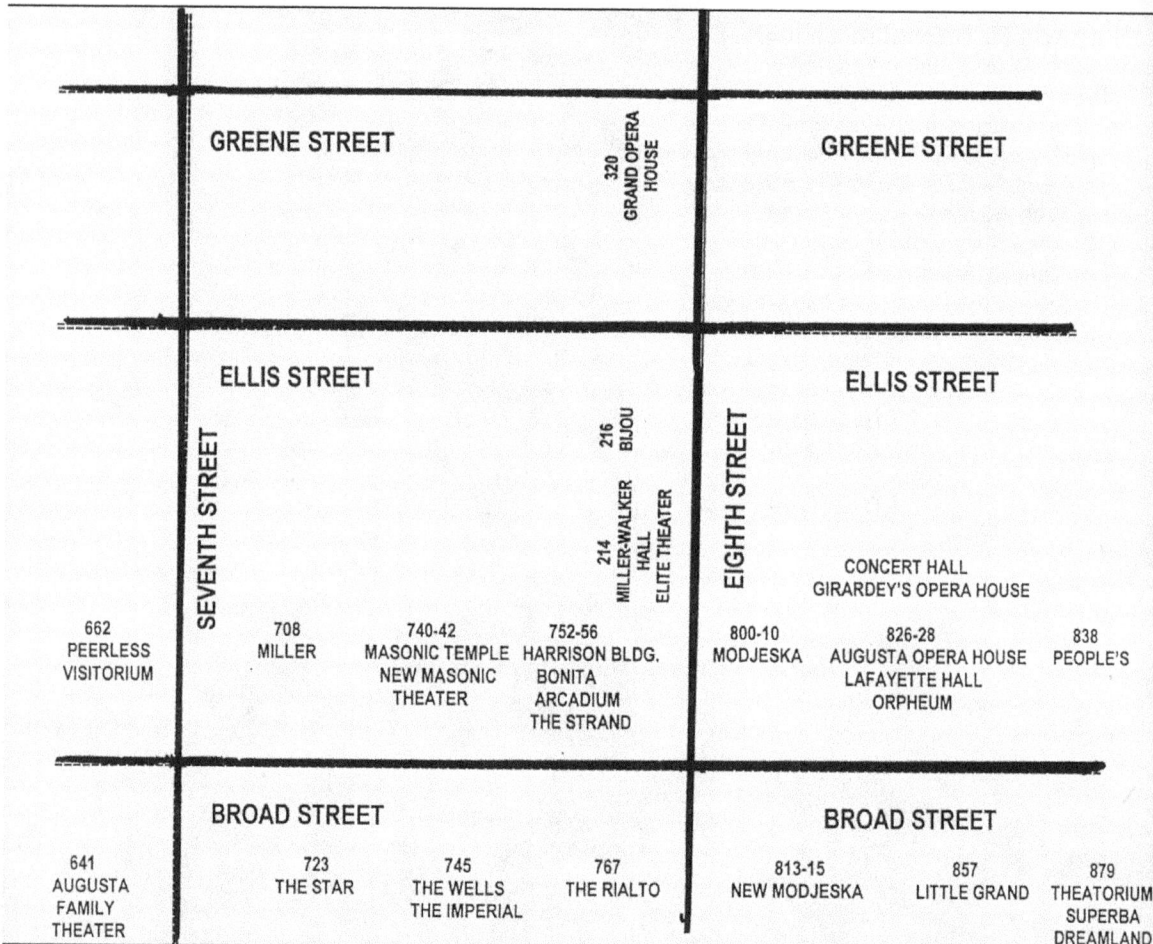

NOTABLE THEATERS. This map created by the author shows notable Augusta stage and movie theaters in the 19th and 20th centuries. Several theaters changed names. The Concert Hall/Girardey's Opera House building in the 800 block of Broad Street had entrances on both Ellis and Broad Streets. Scores of the best-known names in American entertainment history performed within these few blocks.

(*above, left*) SIGN OF THE TIMES. It looked like curtains for the once-great Modjeska Theater when Bob Lollar took down its sign on August 19, 1986. But the theater would take on a new life in the early 21st century as a popular nightclub for the "in" crowd. (Photo by Judy Ondrey; Courtesy *The Augusta Chronicle*.)

(*above, right*) LENOX TORN DOWN. The Lenox didn't have such a nice fate with the wrecking ball bringing down the building on September 15, 1978. Part of Augusta's rich African-American entertainment history was lost forever. (Photo by Rickey Pittman; Courtesy *The Augusta Chronicle*.)

LENOX REMAINS. All that remained of the Lenox entranceway in the late 1980s was this broken ceramic tile at its entranceway. (Photo by Don Rhodes.)

CATTLE DRIVE. It wasn't so far-fetched for Augustans to see longhorn cattle being driven on Broad Street, as with this Augusta Futurity horse and carriage parade on January 17, 1993. Legend has it that Broad Street intentionally was created wide to make room for cattle being driven to the Lower Market at Fifth and Broad Streets in Augusta's pioneer days. The annual Futurity event has become one of the largest equestrian parades in the Southeast. (Photo by Dan Doughtie; Courtesy *The Augusta Chronicle*.)

Four

PARADES, FESTIVALS, AND OTHER FUN

Augustans have loved big celebrations for two centuries, including the Festival of St. John the Evangelist, observed annually in the 1780s by members of the Masonic Lodge Columbia. Grand celebrations for visiting dignitaries began with planned activities for President George Washington during his May 18–21, 1791, visit when Augusta was the capital of the state.

By the early 1800s, circuses regularly came to town and held parades on Broad Street. And in 1888, the National Exposition (billed as "a miniature world on 93 acres") was held November 2 through December 18 on Druid Park Avenue where Paine College now exists.

Throughout the 1800s and 1900s, other celebrations included fairs, parades, arts festivals, church anniversaries, sporting events, and other fun times.

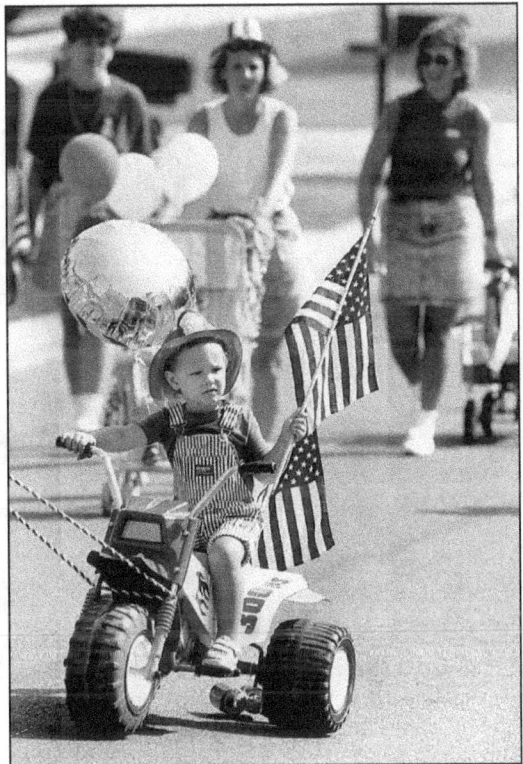

KID ON TRI-WHEELER. Michael Shane Baura, two years old, pedals his three-wheeler in Augusta's Carson subdivision for a neighborhood Fourth of July parade on July 4, 1990. (Photo by Blake Madden; Courtesy *The Augusta Chronicle*.)

SINGING IN THE PARK. Bicentennial Park (the middle of Broad Street between Sixth and Tenth Streets) has featured many entertainment offerings, including this concert by the Sweet Adelines on October 13, 1976. One concert series held at noon on Wednesdays in the late 1970s was the idea of Jeannie Cross Allen, Miss Georgia of 1968 and a finalist in the Miss America competition. (Photo by Jim Middleton; Courtesy *The Augusta Chronicle*.)

PAINE COLLEGE HOMECOMING PARADE. Glenn Hills High School head majorette Laneequa Truesdell, left, demonstrates a baton routine to fellow majorettes at the start of the Paine College Homecoming Parade on February 13, 1993. (Photo by Rudy Nyhoff; Courtesy *The Augusta Chronicle*.)

54

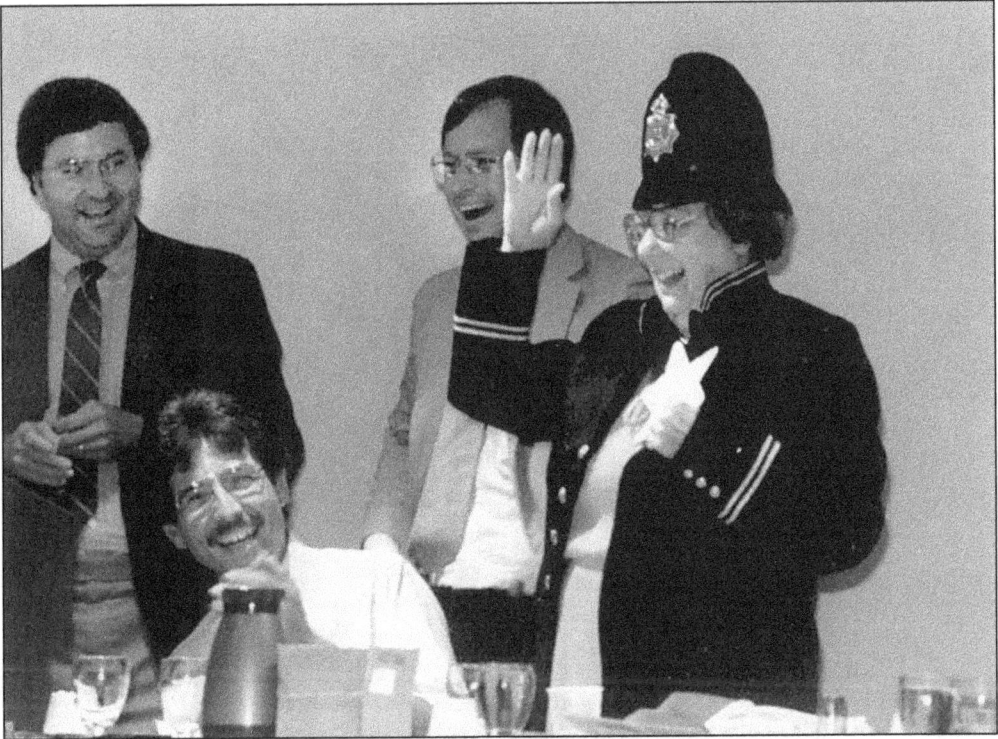

POLITICAL ROASTS. One unusual form of entertainment in Augusta has been political roasts, especially a series of "Turkey Shoots" sponsored by the Sigma Delta Chi organization for professional journalists. This retirement roast on July 12, 1984, in the Civic Center was for Margaret Twiggs, longtime writer for the *Augusta Herald* and *The Augusta Chronicle*. Laughing, from left to right, are Dayton Sherrouse, then executive-director of the Augusta-Richmond County Planning Commission; roast emcee Bob Young, later mayor of Augusta; and Stovall Walker, an Augusta city councilman who was Twiggs's neighbor, and honoree Twiggs. (Photo by Don Rhodes.)

COTTON PARADE. Two farmers sit high atop their bales of cotton as they pass Seventh and Broad Streets in the annual Cotton Parade. This photo was taken in 1908 by John C. McAuliffe, editor of the *Augusta Herald*. (Courtesy Joseph M. Lee III.)

FESTIVAL OF TREES. The Festival of Trees celebration, organized by the Junior League of Augusta, moved from Regency Mall to the Port Royal shopping mall and then to the Augusta Museum of History. Here, on Children's Day of the festival at Port Royal on November 20, 1991, one man band performer Henry Tippins shows 5-year-old Rob Lamb of Floyd Graham Elementary School how to play a washboard. (Photo by Margaret Sellers; Courtesy *The Augusta Chronicle*.)

SACRED HEART EVENTS. People in the late 1970s actually were considering tearing down the former Sacred Heart Catholic Church building. The church had been dedicated on December 2, 1900, and had its last Catholic service on July 4, 1971. But enter philanthropist Peter S. Knox Jr., who put up the money to restore the church to its former glory. The reborn Sacred Heart Cultural Center became host to Masters Tournament–related parties, the Christmas Afternoon at Sacred Heart series, the Evening in Ireland parties, garden shows, chamber music and choral concerts, and the first WKXC Million Pennies For Kids Guitar Pull. (Photo by Margaret Moore; Courtesy *The Augusta Chronicle*.)

MILITARY ON PARADE. An estimated 30,000 Pennsylvania soldiers of the 28th Division of the U.S. Army based at Camp Hancock (now Daniel Field airport) marched from their base to downtown Augusta on February 22, 1918, and then marched back. Their band played the division's adopted battle song, "Onward Christian Soldier," as well as "Dixie." The parade, said to be five miles long, took two hours to pass any given point. (Courtesy the Augusta Museum of History.)

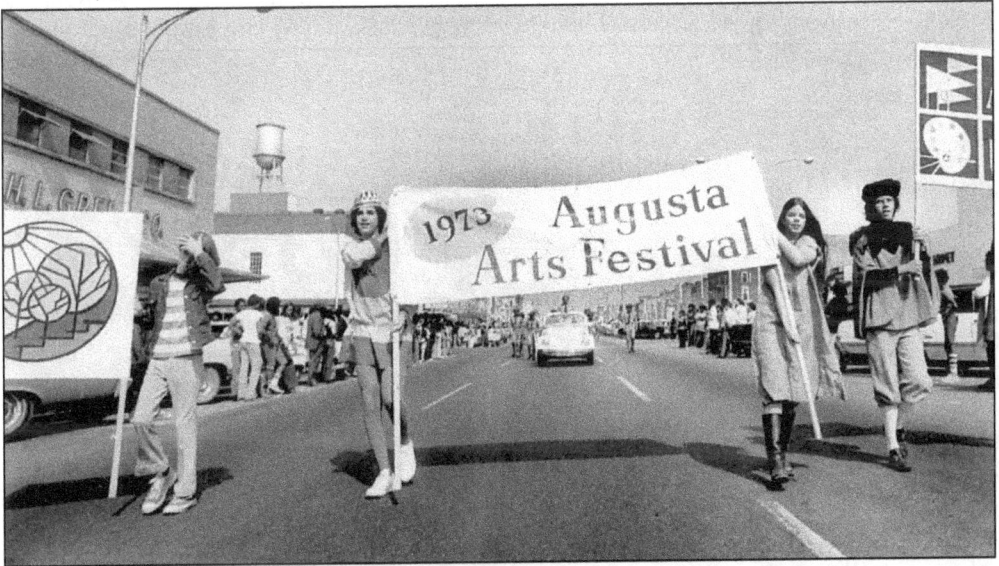

ARTS FESTIVAL PARADE. Thousands of volunteers in the early 1970s, inspired by community activist Nancy Anderson, cleared out thick brush and foliage on the north side of the downtown levee to create Oglethorpe Park, the forerunner of Riverwalk. The revitalized area became the scene of several arts festivals. This parade on May 19, 1973, helped launch that year's festival. Note the sign at left showing the Oglethorpe Park logo. (Courtesy *The Augusta Chronicle*.)

MASTERS PARADE BALLOONS. For several years, the Masters golf tournament was promoted with a downtown parade when it was difficult to give tickets away. One special parade feature was the release of balloons such as this one on April 4, 1961, in front of the Georgia Railroad Bank at Seventh and Broad Streets. (Photo by Morgan Fitz; Courtesy Fitz-Symms Studio.)

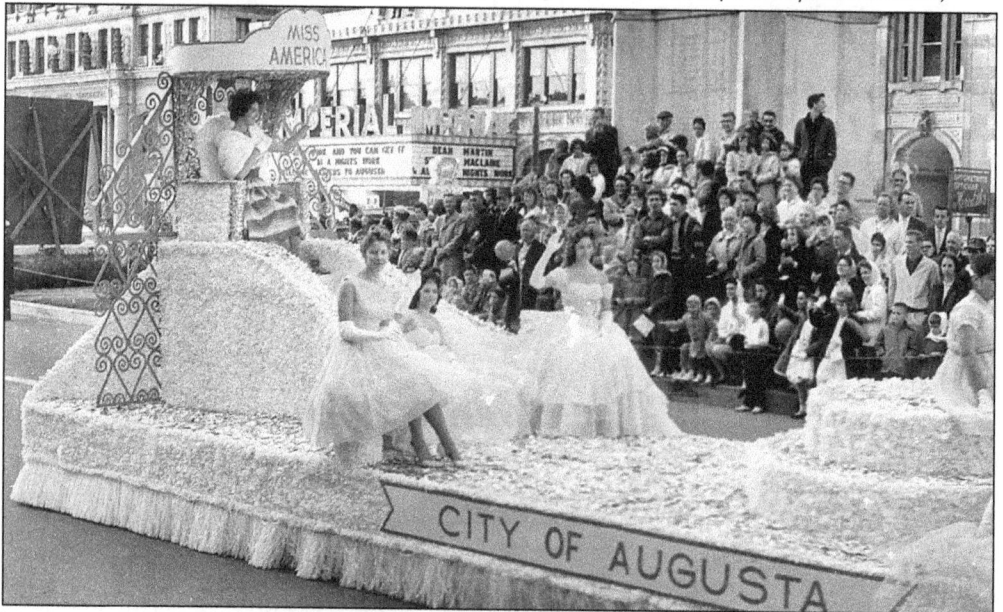

MISS AMERICA FLOAT. The 1960 Miss America, Lynda Lee Mead of Natchez, Mississippi, rode on the City of Augusta's float during the Masters Week parade on April 5, 1961. (Photo by Morgan Fitz; Courtesy Fitz-Symms Studio.)

BICENTENNIAL FLOAT. This float was part of one of three parades (May 14–16, 1935) celebrating the city of Augusta's bicentennial. Georgia governor Eugene Talmadge rode with Mayor Richard E. Allen Jr. in the third and final parade on May 16. (Courtesy the Augusta Museum of History.)

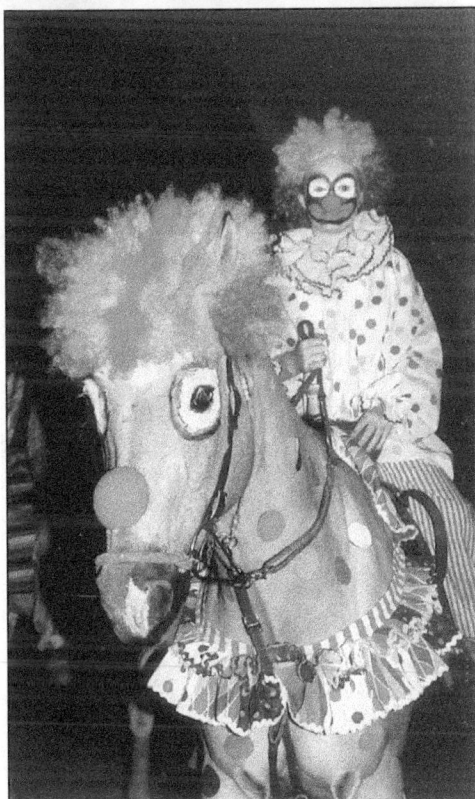

TRICK OR TROT. One of the more unusual events to take place annually in Augusta is the Trick or Trot competition on Halloween night during the National Barrel Horse Association World Championships in the Augusta-Richmond County Civic Center, with riders dressing up themselves and their horses. This was taken during the 1996 Trick or Trot. (Photo by Patrick King; Courtesy Morris Communications Co.)

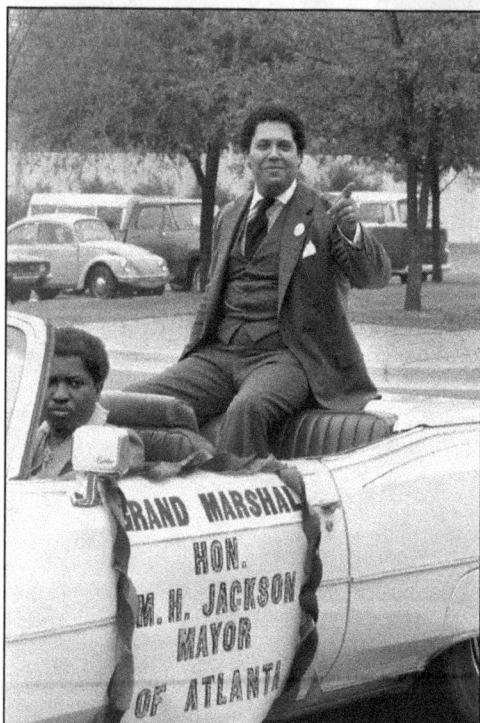

CARL EDWARD SANDERS. Politicians can also be entertaining. Thousands turned out on Broad Street on September 24, 1962, to congratulate native son Carl Sanders on being elected governor of Georgia. Riding with him were his son, Carl Sanders Jr.; wife, Betty; and daughter, Betty Foy. Governor Sanders was the only Augustan in the 20th century to be elected governor of Georgia. His first elected office was president of his freshman class at Richmond Academy. Governor Sanders developed Augusta State University into a four-year college and brought about the state's public broadcasting system. Georgia PBS station WCES in Wrens bears his initials. (Courtesy *The Augusta Chronicle*.)

MAYNARD JACKSON. The grand marshal for the Augusta Black Festival Parade on March 29, 1980, was Atlanta mayor Maynard Jackson, who rode on this convertible. Atlanta's main airport was renamed in 2003 to honor Jackson. (Photo by Phillip Powell; Courtesy *The Augusta Chronicle*.)

STROM THURMOND. One politician who truly loved parades was U.S. senator Strom Thurmond of Edgefield, South Carolina, seen here at 91 riding horseback in the Ridge Peach Festival Parade in Trenton, South Carolina, on June 18, 1994. He also took part regularly in other South Carolina festivals such as the Chitlin' Strut in Salley and the Heritage Festival in Beech Island. (Photo by Ron Cockerille; Courtesy *The Augusta Chronicle*.)

LESTER MADDOX ON BICYCLE. You could always count on something amusing when Governor (and later Lieutenant Governor) Lester Garfield Maddox came to town. Here on October 15, 1972, he demonstrates his talent for riding a bicycle backwards. (Photo by Lee Downing; Courtesy *The Augusta Chronicle*.)

SANTA ON FLOAT. What would Christmas be without a good parade welcoming Santa Claus to town, even if he does have to hurry back to the North Pole to deliver presents on Christmas Eve? (Photo by Morgan Fitz; Courtesy Fitz-Symms Studio.)

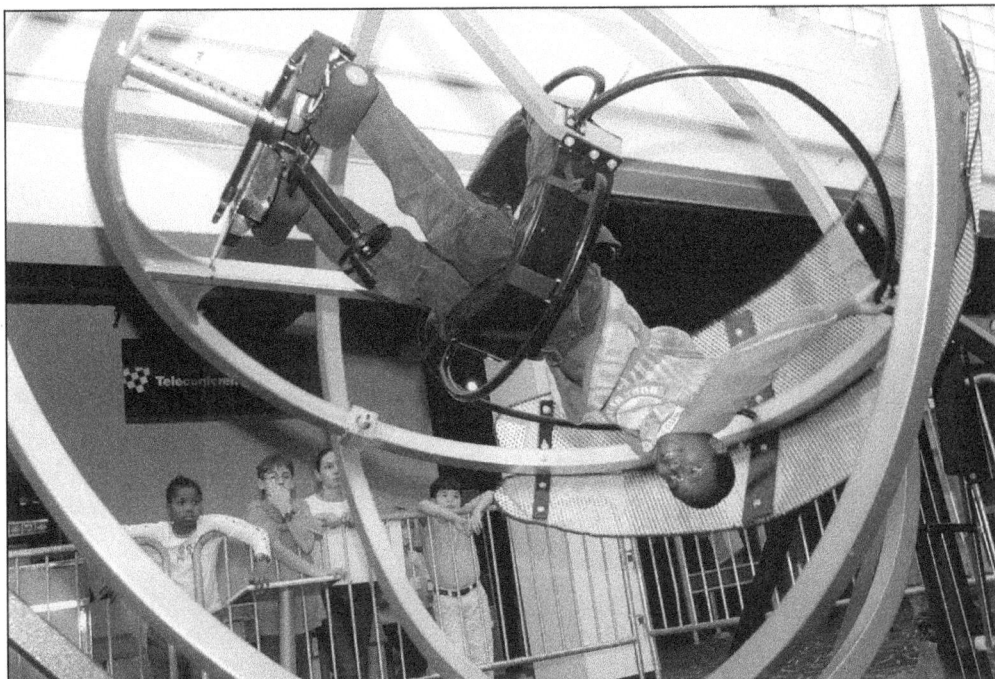

DISCOVERING FORT DISCOVERY. Demanti O'Bryant, age 11, of North Augusta, South Carolina, plays on the human gyro at the National Science Center's Fort Discovery on February 9, 2002. Roughly 8,000 children and adults attended the public opening of the educational facility on April 26, 1997, in the Port Royal building at Augusta's Riverwalk. The center's 250-seat Paul S. Simon Discovery Theater later opened on August 9, 1997. (Photo by Chris Thelen; Courtesy *The Augusta Chronicle*.)

DAY IN THE COUNTRY. Country music star Mel McDaniel arrived in his custom touring bus through a sea of thousands of people at the fifth annual Day in the Country music festival on May 6, 1990, at Augusta Riverfront Marina. Also on the show were Wild Rose, Vern Gosdin, and Mark Collie. (Photo by Don Rhodes.)

FAIR MIDWAY. Sunny days in the fall bring out thousands of Augusta area folks to the annual Exchange Club of Augusta fair. The fair is held on the former site of Warren Park baseball field, where Ty Cobb first played professional ball for the Augusta Tourists in 1904. (Photo by Don Rhodes.)

ROCKIN' WITH LEON. Playing at the Augusta Black Festival on April 8, 1981, was the Soul Burners band featuring Leon Austin, left, on organ. Austin, a childhood friend of James Brown, rocked Augusta in the 1950s with his group Leon Austin and The Buicks. (Photo by Lannis Waters; Courtesy *The Augusta Chronicle*.)

64

JAMES BROWN COMES HOME. One of the biggest turnouts on Broad Street was when entertainer James Brown, who had been living in New York state, returned to the city of his childhood for James Brown Day on February 4, 1969. He soon afterward moved back to Augusta after buying a house on The Hill on Walton Way Extension. Brown is in the car. (Photo by Jim King; Courtesy *The Augusta Chronicle*.)

FOURTH OF JULY FIREWORKS. The crowd reacts to loud noises at the Fourth of July parade on Broad Street in 1991. (Photo by Margaret Moore Sellers; Courtesy *The Augusta Chronicle*.)

JERRY HARRIS. One of Augusta's best-liked and most talented entertainers was Jerry Harris, shown on December 21, 1983 playing in the Eagle's Nest nightclub atop the Augusta Hilton (later the Landmark and Ramada Hotels). He was the pianist at the Lenox Theater and played at the Ship Ahoy restaurant on Broad for many years. His sister, Rose Sanders Creque, was opera star Jessye Norman's first formal voice coach. His nephew, Tim Sanders, now plays in the popular PlayBack band. (Photo by Shaun Stanley; Courtesy *The Augusta Chronicle*.)

ETTA JONES. Born November 25, 1928, in Aiken, South Carolina, this memorable singer died of cancer October 16, 2001, at age 72 at her home in Mount Vernon, New York. Her High Tone Records album, *Etta Jones Sings the Songs of Lady Day*, was released the day she died. In early 2002, Prestige Records released an 18-song CD, *The Best of Etta Jones (The Prestige Singles)*. (Album Cover, *The Best of Etta Jones*, Courtesy Fantasy Inc. Prestige Records].)

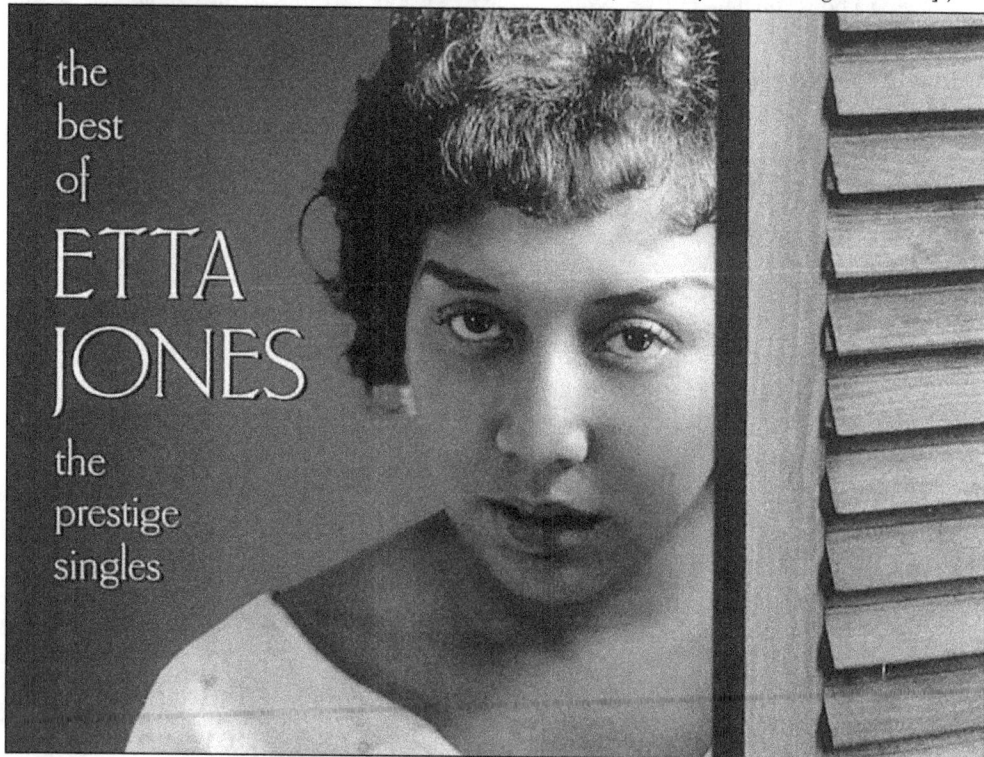

the
best
of
ETTA
JONES
the
prestige
singles

Five

HOMETOWN HEROES
AND HEROINES

Creative Augusta area musicians, writers, actors, and others started becoming nationally and internationally known in the 1800s. Early ones would have to include humor writer and University of South Carolina president Augustus Baldwin Longstreet; travel book author Octavia Walton LeVert; and poet, Augusta lawyer, and U.S. Congressman Richard Henry Wilde. Augustan Berry Fleming received nationwide praise for his book The Conqueror's Stone *in 1927, and Erskine Caldwell of Wrens, Georgia, published his first novel,* The Bastard, *in 1929.*

Oliver Hardy, born in Harlem, Georgia, and Butterfly McQueen, born in Tampa, Florida, and raised in Augusta, were two of the first movie stars from the Augusta area. Arthur Lee Simpkins, who entertained Augustans with his Night Hawks band, became one of the first nationally-known recording artists from Augusta.

DIXIE DOOLEY. Dangling from a crane high over Broad Street on October 22, 1979, while escaping from a straitjacket next to the Confederate Memorial figure of Berry Benson, was Augusta magician Dixie Dooley. The son of an Augusta real estate salesman now headlines his own tribute shows to magician Harry Houdini in Las Vegas. (Photo by Jim Middleton; Courtesy *The Augusta Chronicle.*)

OLIVER NORVELL HARDY. The rotund man in the 1929 MGM comedy *Wrong Again* is Oliver Hardy, born January 18, 1892, in Harlem, Georgia. The partner of British-born comic Stan Laurel began making silent movies in 1913 and first appeared with Mr. Laurel in *The Lucky Dog* in 1921. Harlem annually hosts the Oliver Hardy Festival the first Saturday in October. He died August 7, 1957, at age 65. (Courtesy author's collection.)

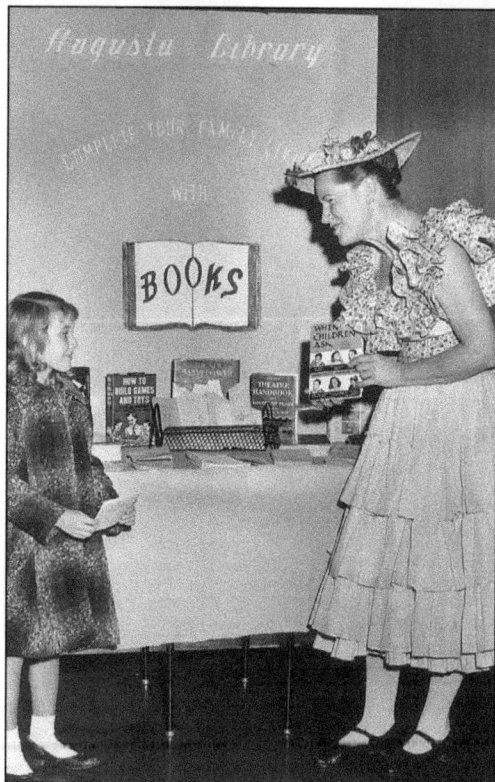

MINNIE PEARL. Sarah Ophelia Colley Cannon, better known as Minnie Pearl, talked with Joan Merritt in the Augusta library on February 11, 1960. The *Grand Ole Opry* star came to Augusta many times for business promotions and shows in Bell Auditorium. She first became "Minnie Pearl" on April 15, 1939, at a Pilot Club convention in the Highland Park Hotel in Aiken, South Carolina. Earlier that day at B.M. Surasky's Department Store in Aiken, she bought the costume that she would wear on her first *Opry* appearance in Ryman Auditorium. (Photo by Morgan Fitz; Courtesy Fitz-Symms Studio.)

JOHNNIE BAILES. Although born in West Virginia, Johnnie Bailes spent almost half of his 71 years in Swainsboro, Georgia, where he was buried December 23, 1989. He was a songwriter and lead vocalist with the Bailes Brothers, regulars on the *Grand Ole Opry* from 1943 to 1946 and co-founders of the *Louisiana Hayride Show* in Shreveport in 1946. He put Little Jimmy Dickens on the air for the first time and helped Webb Pierce and Hank Williams get on the *Hayride* show. He later managed three Augusta-area radio stations owned by Pierce in Georgia: WJAT in Swainsboro, WBRO in Waynesboro, and WSNT in Sandersville. (Courtesy Johnnie Bailes.)

BLIND WILLIE McTELL. William Samuel McTier, who became famous as legendary blues singer Blind Willie McTell, was born near Thomson, Georgia, on May 5, 1901. His recordings, begun in late 1927 with Victor Records, included his classic composition, "Statesboro Blues." During the Christmas season of 1933, he met Ruthy Kate Williams in Augusta. They applied for a marriage license on January 10, 1934, at the Aiken County, South Carolina Courthouse and were married by a notary public the next day. The McTells performed and recorded together, sharing stages with legendary artists such as Louis Armstrong, Cab Calloway, and Bessie Smith. He died on August 19, 1959, and Kate died October 3, 1991. (Courtesy *The Augusta Chronicle.*)

KAREN BROWN. This Augusta native was named artistic director of the Oakland Ballet in California in April 2000. Brown, a graduate of Aquinas High School in Augusta, was dancing with the Augusta Ballet in Richmond, Virginia, when Karen Shook, co-director of the Dance Theater of Harlem in New York City spotted her and offered her a scholarship. She was with the Dance Theatre of Harlem from 1973 to 1995 and became its principal dancer. Here she rehearses with the Dance Theater's Keith Saunders. (Courtesy Dance Theatre of Harlem.)

HULK HOGAN. Terry Gene Bollea, who became world famous as professional wrestler Hulk Hogan, weighed 10 pounds and 7 ounces when born to Peter and Ruth Bollea in Augusta's St. Joseph Hospital on August 11, 1953. His father was a pipefitter building the Savannah River atomic energy plant. Bollea's family then lived at Pecan Grove trailer court in Aiken, South Carolina. The family moved to Tampa, Florida, where teenaged Terry began bodybuilding in 1967. He returned to Augusta and the Whippin' Post nightclub in 1975 as a bass guitar player for the rock band Rukkus. This photo was taken during a wrestling match in the Augusta-Richmond County Civic Center on November 11, 1989. (Photo by Eric Olig; Courtesy *The Augusta Chronicle*.)

DANNY GLOVER. Movie actor Danny Glover, often the co-star in Mel Gibson's action films, signs a photo for Lamar Elementary School student Kentae Green after speaking at the school on February 9, 1994. Glover's mother, Carrie, was born in Augusta and was a graduate of Paine College. Glover spent many summers growing up on his grandparents' farm off U.S. Highway 1 between Wrens and Louisville. (Photo by Matthew Craig; Courtesy *The Augusta Chronicle*.)

PETE DRAKE. Roddis Franklin "Pete" Drake was born in Augusta on October 8, 1932, and died in Nashville, Tennessee, on July 29, 1988. His father was a Pentecostal preacher in Augusta. Drake became a recording producer, record company founder, and musician whose steel guitar is heard on hundreds of hit recordings, including Lynn Anderson's "Rose Garden," Charlie Rich's "Behind Closed Doors," George Harrison's "My Sweet Lord," Bob Dylan's "Lay Lady Lay," and Tammy Wynette's "Stand By Your Man." He produced Ringo Starr's best-selling *Beaucoup of Blues* album in mid-1970, which marked the first time a Beatle had recorded in the United States. (Courtesy Pete Drake.)

71

JAYNE MANSFIELD. The glamorous film actress Jayne Mansfield in 1952 was 19 years old and living at 161 Damascus Road as the wife of Fort Gordon–based Lt. Paul Mansfield. She often caught a bus into Augusta to take acting and singing lessons. She was back in Augusta on May 18, 1966, to headline a show in Bell Auditorium with Minnie Pearl, Sonny James & The Southern Gentlemen, Johnny PayCheck, and Tommy Cash. And she returned the same month to perform May 26–27 in the Celebrity Room at the Whisk-A-Go-Go nightclub on Broad Street. (Courtesy *The Augusta Chronicle*.)

DUB TAYLOR. Seen here, from left to right, from the television series *Hee Haw* is Walter Clarence "Dub" Taylor Jr. wearing a Derby hat and series regulars Gailard Sartain and Lula Roman. Taylor, who died October 3, 1994, at age 87, lived in Augusta from age five through 13. His father was a cotton broker in the Cotton Exchange. Taylor became a close friend of neighbor Ty Cobb Jr., the son of the baseball player. He later appeared in more than 500 movies, including *Auntie Mame, Parrish, How the West Was Won, The Wild Bunch, No Time For Sergeants*, and *Bonnie & Clyde*. (Courtesy the Nashville Network Cable Network.)

LARRY JON WILSON. The early 1970s saw the emergence in Augusta of distinctive vocalist Larry Jon Wilson, signed to Monument Records in Nashville in 1973. He became a "singer's singer" admired by legends like Willie Nelson, Waylon Jennings, Tammy Wynette, Kris Kristofferson, Larry Gatlin, and Mickey Newbury. His deep voice is heard regularly on the Turner South cable TV network announcing upcoming programs. He has performed in all the "in" nightclubs, such as The Other End in New York City, The Cellar Door near Washington, D.C., and The Exit Inn in Nashville. (Courtesy Monument Records.)

JOSEPH JENNINGS. As composer, arranger, and director since 1984 of Chanticleer, the only full-time classical vocal ensemble in the nation, Joseph Jennings has won multiple Grammy Awards. He graduated from Augusta's Richmond Academy in 1971 and grew up playing piano on Sunday mornings for Macedonia Baptist Church on Wrightsboro Road. He was influenced musically by his mother, Doris, and by his father, Warren, who has collected more than 3,000 albums. His father bought him a piano when he was six and later a B-3 organ. (Courtesy Warren Jennings.)

73

TERRI GIBBS. Augusta's Butler High School on March 23, 1983, dedicated its new music complex to Teresa Fay Gibbs Daughtry, who also performed for the dedicatory audience. She grew up singing gospel and country music in the Augusta area and graduated from Butler High in 1972. Her first MCA Records single, "Somebody's Knockin'," became an international music sensation in 1981. That same year, she became the first artist to win the Country Music Association's Horizon Award for upcoming performers. She also won the Academy of Country Music's Best New Female Vocalist Award. (Photo by Judy Ondrey; Courtesy *The Augusta Chronicle*.)

LEON EVERETTE. Born Leon Baughman on March 27, 1949, in Aiken, South Carolina, Leon Everette was reared in Queens, New York. He was living in Ward, South Carolina, near Aiken, when signed by True Records in Nashville. That resulted in his hit tribute single to Elvis Presley, "Goodbye King of Rock and Roll." He had other hit singles with Orlando, RCA, and Mercury/PolyGram Records, appeared on network television shows, and toured the United States and foreign countries. (Courtesy PolyGram Records.)

MILLIE JACKSON. Born and raised in Thomson, Georgia, Millie Jackson once sneaked off to see blues legend B.B. King at an outdoor concert in Richmond County. She was his opening act years later in Bell Auditorium. Many of her more than 25 albums—recorded in such diverse locations as London, New York, and Nashville—have gone gold (sales of 250,000 copies or more), and she has recorded soulful duets with the likes of Elton John and Isaac Hayes. Her 1973 single, "It Hurts So Good," was heard in the movie *Cleopatra Jones*. (Courtesy Millie Jackson.)

ARTHUR LEE SIMPKINS. Popular tenor Arthur Lee Simpkins performed at black and white parties in the 1930s and 1940s with his band, the Night Hawks. The former Georgia Railroad Bank porter had a worldwide hit single with "Trees," a song set to the Joyce Kilmer poem. He spoke six languages and was guest soloist at the 1952 National Democratic Convention in Chicago. (Courtesy *The Augusta Chronicle*.)

THE SWANEE QUINTET. The Swanee Quintet, which comedian Bill Cosby called one of his favorite Apollo Theatre acts, has performed in almost every state, including venues such as Carnegie Hall and Madison Square Garden. The group began as a trio with Charlie Barnwell, Rufus Washington, and William Crawford singing together in Georgia and South Carolina in 1944. They soon added James "Big Red" Anderson and Rubin Willingham to become the Swanee Quintet in 1946. Shown are, from left to right, (front row) Gus Mims, Johnny Mims, and Johnny Jones; (back row) Percy Griffin, with original members Anderson and Barnwell. (Courtesy the Swanee Quintet.)

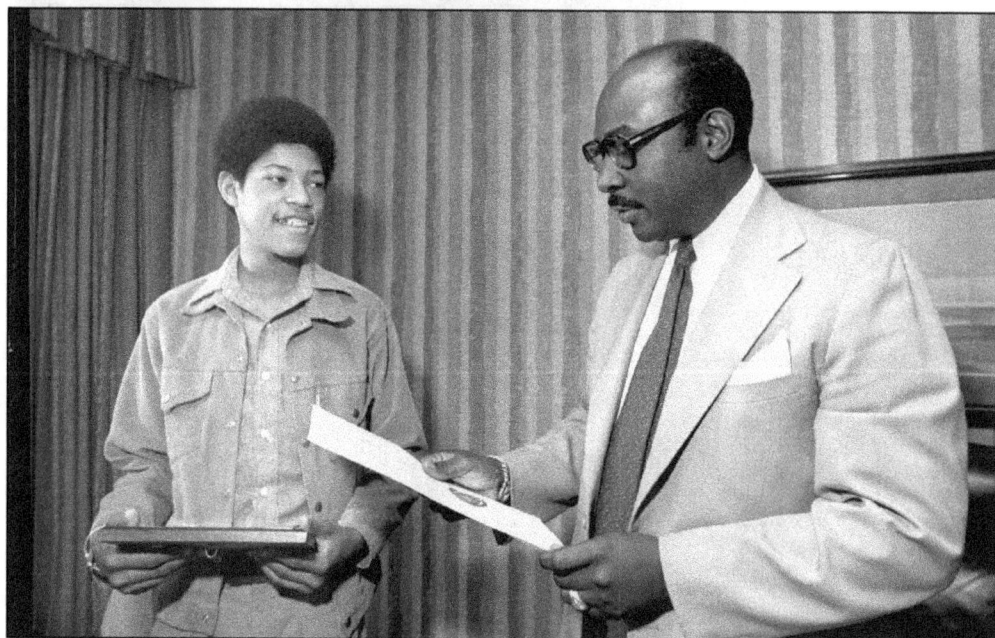

LAURENCE FISHBURNE III. *Matrix* movie star Laurence Fishburne III was born to John and Hattie Fishburne in Augusta's old University Hospital on July 30, 1961. He was nominated for an Oscar for playing Ike Turner in *What's Love Got To Do With It* and won a 1992 Tony Award as Best Featured Actor for *Two Trains Running*. He was just a 13-year-old boy on June 13, 1975, greeting Edward M. McIntyre, chairman of the Richmond County Commission, who proclaimed "Lawrence Fishburne III Day" in Richmond County to honor his feature film debut in *Cornbread, Earl and Me.* (Photo by Mike Craven; Courtesy *The Augusta Chronicle*.)

JAMES BROWN. James Brown was born in rural Barnwell County, South Carolina, near Elko, on May 3, 1933. He is probably the most honored person in Augusta's history with four special days held in his honor: February 4, 1969, with a parade on Broad Street; June 28, 1986, at Augusta Riverfront Marina; November 20, 1993, as seen in this photo for the renaming of Ninth (Campbell) Street in his honor; and November 15, 2003, at Augusta Common to add two more blocks of Ninth Street in his name and to announce that a statue will be erected in his honor. (Photo by Rudy Nyhoff; Courtesy *The Augusta Chronicle*.)

FAVORITE TEACHER. Even though James Brown dropped out of Silas X. Floyd Elementary School in the fifth grade, he has always praised former teacher Laura Garvin (seen with him on May 2, 1972, the day before Brown's 39th birthday). He has been one of the industry's loudest voices urging young people to get a good education, especially with his hit single "(Stay In School) Don't Be A Dropout." He and his wife, Tomi Rae, plan to create a music education program in the old Silas X. Floyd school. (Photo by Lee Downing; Courtesy *The Augusta Chronicle*.)

FLO CARTER. This Augusta pioneer of rockabilly music is shown here, from left to right, with her band The Rockets: Chuck Conners, Don Carter, Al Sullivan, and Tom Edenfield. Mrs. Carter in the 1950s co-hosted the *Today In Dixie* variety show at noon weekdays on WJBF-TV. She regularly sang duets on the program with "Jimmy" Nabors, later famous as TV character Gomer Pyle. She had her own gospel music show in the 1980s on WJBF featuring her current band, The Sounds of Joy. She has sung in New York City's Central Park, on The Mall in Washington, D.C., and with many Augusta groups, including the Augusta Concert Band and the Augusta Symphony. She was honored in 1997 by the Greater Augusta Arts Council as Artist of the Year. (Courtesy Flo Carter.)

AMY GRANT. Grammy Award–winning rock and Christian singer Amy Grant was born in St. Joseph Hospital on November 25, 1960, to Dr. Burton Paine Grant and Gloria Grant. Her father spent two years as a doctor at Dwight D. Eisenhower Army Medical Center and then did his residency in radiology at the Medical College of Georgia. The family lived at 2263 Raleigh Drive in the Forest Acres subdivision before moving to Nashville, Tennessee. Miss Grant was signed by Word Music's Myrrh Label in 1976. She expanded in 1991 to secular pop, scoring a hit with "Baby, Baby." She is married to country superstar Vince Gill. (Courtesy Word Music.)

JESSYE NORMAN. The great opera star, shown here in Augusta on May 1, 2002, was born September 15, 1945, to Silas and Janie King Norman in Augusta's old University Hospital. She grew up at 1444 Forest Avenue listening to Saturday afternoon broadcasts of the Metropolitan Opera while cleaning her family's house. She won her first talent contest singing in Augusta's Mount Calvary Baptist Church, where her father was superintendent of the Sunday School classes. She sang for Queen Elizabeth II on the queen's 60th birthday, at President Ronald Reagan's 1985 inauguration, in Paris for the 200th anniversary of Bastille Day, and at the funeral of Jacqueline Kennedy Onassis. The amphitheater at Riverwalk Augusta is named in her honor. (Photo by Michael Holohan; Courtesy *The Augusta Chronicle*.)

CARL SMITH. Augustans knew country music superstar Carl Smith in two stages of his life. He lived in a boarding house across from Bell Auditorium in the 1950s, making local appearances and singing on WGAC radio live broadcasts with the Smokey Mountaineers. He became a country music legend selling thousands of recordings. But he returned to Augusta throughout the 1980s and 1990s as a cutting horse competitor and board member of The Augusta Futurity. He was inducted into the Country Music Association's Hall of Fame in 2003. (Courtesy Columbia Records and *The Augusta Chronicle*.)

SUTTON FOSTER. This Tony Award winner (Best Actress 2002 as Millie Dillmount in *Thoroughly Modern Millie*) is shown here rehearsing in September of 1985 her title role in the Augusta Players' production of *Annie*. She was born in Statesboro, Georgia, but she received much of her early stage training in Augusta. The daughter of Bob and Helen Foster was a student at South Columbia Elementary School at that time. She only had a supporting role in the Augusta Players' Youth Theater production of *Grease* in April of 1987, but she later would have the starring role of Sandy in *Grease* on Broadway. Other Augusta roles were in *A Christmas Carol* (1982) and also *Lighted Windows*, *The Sound of Music, Not Even A Mouse*, and *It's The Night Before Christmas* (1986). (Photo by Lannis Waters; Courtesy *The Augusta Chronicle*.)

FAITH PRINCE. Actress Faith Prince was born to Keith and Gloria Prince in St. Joseph's Hospital in Augusta on August 6, 1957. She won a 1992 Tony Award as Best Actress in a Musical for playing Miss Adelaide in *Guys and Dolls*. She also was nominated in 2001 for another Tony for her starring role in the revival of *Bells Are Ringing*. She was raised in Lynchburg, Virginia, but returned often to Augusta to visit her grandparents Cleon and Ruth Prince. Her television credits include recurring roles on *Spin City* and *Now And Again*. (Courtesy *The Augusta Chronicle*.)

THE LEWIS FAMILY. This musical group from Lincolnton, Georgia, is known as America's "First Family of Bluegrass-Gospel Music." Shown here at the old Savannah River Lock & Dam are, from left to right, Roy "Pop" Lewis, Wallace Lewis, "Little Roy" Lewis, Miggie Lewis, Polly Lewis Copsey, and Janis Lewis Phillips. The dress Polly is wearing is now on display in the Georgia Music Hall of Fame. Also now performing with the group are Travis Lewis and Lewis Phillips. Their fans have included Elvis Presley, First Lady Mamie Eisenhower, Chet Atkins, Roy Clark, and Vince Gill. The family was inducted into the Georgia Music Hall of Fame in 1992. (Courtesy the Lewis Family.)

HUGH BEAUMONT. Actor Hugh Beaumont may have been Beaver Cleaver's dad, Ward Cleaver, for seven years in the classic television series Leave It To Beaver, but he was a real-life dad to Mark Beaumont, whom he visited often at Mark's home in Aiken, South Carolina. He even directed the play Private Lives in Aiken in the winter of 1980. Hugh then owned a 37-acre island in Minnesota that he regarded as his own home. This photo was taken in May of 1981, the month of Mark's birthday (May 9). Hugh died a year later on May 14, 1982. (Photo by Lannis Waters; Courtesy The Augusta Chronicle.)

JANELLE AND FABIO. Janelle Williams Taylor, resident of Grovetown, Georgia, is shown here with supermodel Fabio, who posed for the cover paintings of several of her lusty historical romance novels. Her more than 35 books have sold in excess of 24 million copies and have made *The New York Times* best seller lists seven times. They have been translated into the languages of more than 25 countries. The native of Athens, Georgia, moved to Augusta after marrying Michael Taylor. She worked three years in medical research in pharmacology and physiology at Medical College of Georgia before becoming a full-time writer. Her first book, *Savage Ecstasy*, was published in September 1981. Her 24th, *Promise Me Forever*, was the first in which she used Augusta as a story locale. (Courtesy Michael Taylor.)

CLIFFORD "BALDY" BALDOWSKI. This famous political cartoonist was born in 1917 in Augusta. He earned a Bronze Star during World War II and became an Air Force Reserve colonel. He returned to Augusta in 1946 after the war and became the editorial cartoonist for *The Augusta Chronicle*. It was in Augusta that he began signing his *Chronicle* cartoons as "Baldy." He left the *Chronicle* to work briefly for the *Miami Herald*. He joined *The Atlanta Constitution* in 1950 and, over 30 years, created roughly 15,000 cartoons. He retired in 1992 and died on September 27, 1999. Thousands of his cartoons are in the University of Georgia library collection. (Photo by Don Rhodes.)

EDISON MARSHALL. Novelist Edison Tesla Marshall, seen here with his books on January 27, 1962, served in the U.S. Army as a public relations officer, which brought him to Camp Hancock in Augusta. He met Agnes Sharp Flythe of Augusta and married her in 1920. His first historical romance novel, *Benjamin Blake*, was published in 1941. It was an instant success and turned into the movie *Son of Fury*, starring Tyrone Power. He proceeded to write almost a novel a year before dying in Augusta on October 30, 1967. Others of his novels include *The Lost Colony* and *Yankee Pasha*. (Breault Newsfoto by Gene Patterson; Courtesy *The Augusta Chronicle*.)

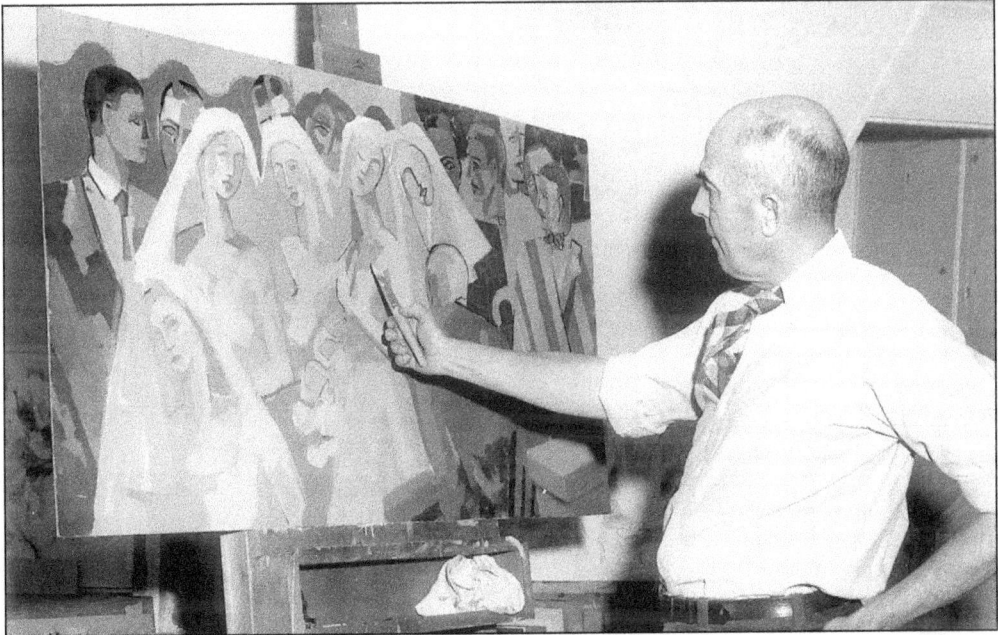

BERRY FLEMING. Nine months before writer and painter Berry Fleming died at age 90 on September 15, 1989, in his native Augusta, the Georgia Senate passed a resolution commending him for his literary contributions to the state. He is shown here at his easel in February of 1961. He authored about 20 books, mostly novels, beginning with his 1927 adventure story, *The Conqueror's Stone*. Berry's best-known novel, *Colonel Effingham's Raid*, was published in 1943. It was a semi-disguised story about the Cracker Party, who had control of the Augusta and Richmond County governments. It was made into a 20th Century Fox movie of the same name starring Savannah-born actor Charles Coburn. (Photo by Robert Symms; Courtesy Fitz-Symms Studio.)

HUNTER FOSTER. This brother of Tony Award winner Sutton Foster also received much of his early stage training in Augusta. He is seen here in 1986 as Rolf with Nancy McKinster in the Augusta Players' musical *The Sound of Music*, singing "Sixteen Going On Seventeen." Foster originated the role of Bobby Strong in the Broadway and Off-Broadway companies of the musical *Urinetown* and, at this book's publication, was starring as Seymour on Broadway in *The Little Shop of Horrors*. His Augusta roles included *Bye, Bye Birdie* (1986 at Evans High School as Conrad Birdie); *Godspell* (1985, winning the Augusta Players Best Supporting Actor, Youth Theater award); *Lighted Windows* (1986); and *Grease* (1987). He also co-starred with Carter Dunbar in *Time To Live*, the WJBF student playhouse production in August of 1987. (Photo by Rudy Nyhoff; Courtesy *The Augusta Chronicle*.)

GINNY WRIGHT. Only two women who had No. 1 duet hit singles with country superstar Jim Reeves when he was alive: Dottie West and Ginny Wright, a longtime resident of the Augusta area. Wright, born in Twin City, Georgia, near Swainsboro, was a star on the *Louisiana Hayride* show when a young Mississippian, Elvis Presley, was making his first *Hayride* appearances. She was named *Cash Box* magazine's Most Promising Country Female Vocalist in 1954. (Courtesy Ginny Wright.)

BUTTERFLY McQUEEN. Longtime Augusta resident and Emmy Award winner Thelma "Butterfly" McQueen is shown here visiting Augusta Mini Theatre students on January 18, 1982. She died in Augusta at 84 on December 22, 1995, from burns suffered when her nightgown caught fire. She had been trying to light a kerosene heater in her small south Augusta home. The actress with the high-pitched voice was best known for playing the slave girl Prissy in the movie *Gone With the Wind*, but she preferred to be known for her many, many other movies, television shows, and stage productions. That included the 1950s ground-breaking television show *Beulah*, one of the first situation comedies to star African-American actors. She worked for a short time for the City of Augusta's recreation department in 1961 teaching acting classes. (Photo by Lannis Waters; Courtesy *The Augusta Chronicle*.)

PAT DYE. Once an athletic star at the Academy of Richmond County, Pat Dye returned there to speak on July 30, 1983. Dye grew up in Blythe, Georgia, in Richmond County with his brothers, Wayne and Nat. All three Dye brothers played football for the University of Georgia under Coach Wally Butts. Pat became head coach of the Auburn University Tigers football team in 1981 and stayed in that position until resigning in 1992. (Photo by Lannis Waters; Courtesy *The Augusta Chronicle*.)

FORREST "SPEC" TOWNS. Forrest "Spec" Towns, who died April 9, 1991, was born in Fitzgerald, Georgia, but grew up in Augusta where his family had moved in 1932. He played football at Richmond Academy but was offered a track and field scholarship to the University of Georgia. Towns set several track records for the school and, in the 1936 Olympics in Berlin, Germany, won the gold medal in the 120-yard hurdles. He became the seventh track and field coach at the University of Georgia in 1938, a position he held until his retirement in 1975. He was inducted into the state of Georgia's Hall of Fame in 1967 and was elected to the U.S. Track and Field Hall of Fame in 1975. (Courtesy *Athens Banner-Herald*.)

Six

IN PURSUIT OF ATHLETIC GREATNESS

More than likely, the first athletic competitions in the Augusta area were among Native Americans from the several local tribes. And probably there was a shooting contest and a canoe race or two among the fur traders and settlers in early 1700s Augusta.

Horse races have been around from the late 1700s, and boating contests were held on the Savannah River and Augusta Canal in the early 1800s. Base Ball games (as written back then) were played in Augusta in the mid-1800s.

There even was a roller skating rink that opened in Augusta in April of 1870.

At the heart of many fun sporting times have been places such as Warren Park, Jennings Stadium, Lake Olmstead, the Augusta Canal, and the International Speedway.

TY COBB. Augustans honored baseball legend Ty Cobb on three special days. This photo was taken at the last on August 29, 1957, in Jennings Stadium off Walton Way. Other special days were August 25, 1905, when he left the Augusta Tourists for the Detroit Tigers, and December 24, 1926, as a show of support in the midst of a baseball scandal. Cobb married Augustan Charlie Lombard in 1908, and they had five children. Cobb owned extensive real estate properties in the Augusta area, including his home at 2425 Williams Street and Ty Cobb Tire Company at Broad and Seventh Streets. He was the first selection for the Baseball Hall of Fame. (Photo by Morgan-Fitz; Courtesy Fitz-Symms Studio.)

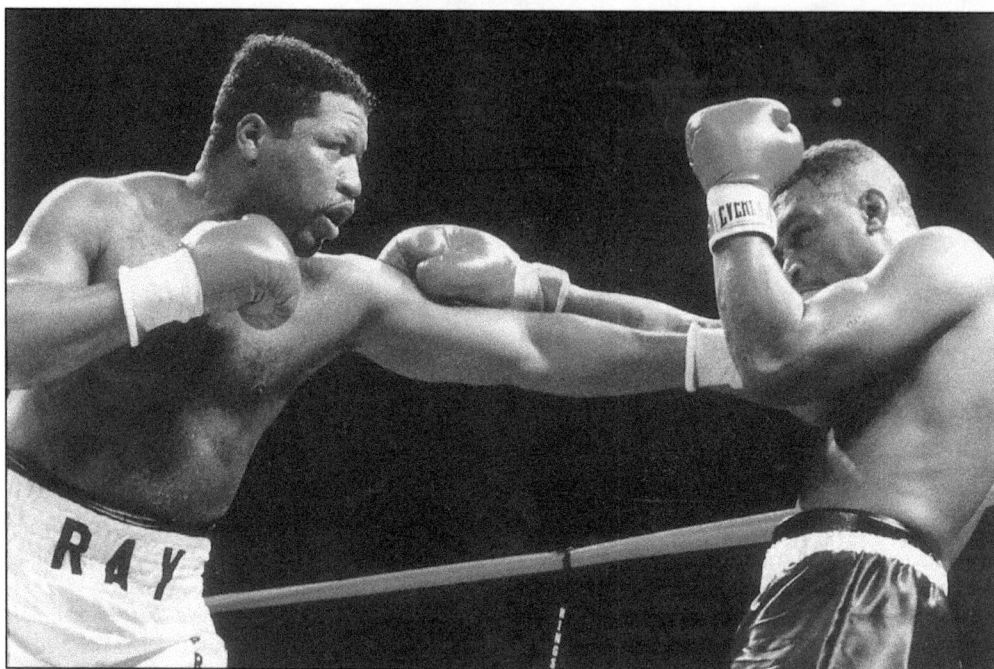

RAY MERCER. Another of Augusta's great athletes was heavyweight boxer Ray Mercer, an Olympic gold medal winner in 1988 in Seoul, Korea. He is shown here in his first professional fight in his hometown (seen on ESPN network), out-boxing Mike Dixon on October 7, 1992, in the Augusta-Richmond County Civic Center. The fight was stopped after the seventh round with Mercer declared the winner. (Photo by Matthew Craig; Courtesy *The Augusta Chronicle*.)

BEAU JACK. Legendary boxer Beau Jack, the subject of many sports profiles, was born Sidney Walker in Waynesboro, Georgia, on April 1, 1921. He was raised in Augusta and became one of the greatest lightweight boxers, twice winning the national title (1942 and 1943). His professional record was 83 wins (including 40 knockouts), 24 losses, and 5 draws. His early years were spent shining shoes at the Augusta National Golf Club. That was where he came to know legendary golfer Bobby Jones, who paid his way north for formal boxing training. He went through $2.5 million and spent his golden years shining shoes at the Fontainebleau Hotel in Miami. He died February 9, 2000, at 78 in a Miami nursing home. (Courtesy *The Augusta Chronicle*.)

LARRY MIZE. The only native Augustan, at the time of this publication, to win the champion's title of the Masters Tournament at the Augusta National is Larry Mize. Here he chips a shot on April 9, 1986. He was born Larry Hogan Mize on September 23, 1958, in St. Joseph's Hospital to Charles and Elizabeth Mize. He captured the 1987 Masters Tournament to become the third Georgia-born golfer to win the Masters. He graduated from Augusta Prep before going to college at Georgia Tech. He turned professional in 1980. (Photo by Randy Hill; Courtesy *The Augusta Chronicle*.)

MITZI EDGE. One of the nation's best female golfers is Mitzi Edge, shown here with her early trophies in October of 1977. She and her brother, Chris, started playing golf with their father, Ken, at Goshen Country Club in south Richmond County in 1966. She was six and Chris was three. She won five tournaments while attending the University of Georgia and was named a first team All-American in 1983 and 1984. She earned a degree at University of Georgia in municipal recreation in 1984. She joined the Ladies Professional Golf Association tour in October of 1984. (Photo by Phillip Powell; Courtesy *The Augusta Chronicle*.)

CHARLIE WATERS. This outstanding athlete, born in 1948, played in five Super Bowls. He showed football skills at North Augusta High School before becoming a star player at Clemson. He was a star defensive back for the Dallas Cowboys (1970–1981) and co-authored with Cliff Harris the book *Tales From The Dallas Cowboys.* He also received some national notoriety for a pinup poster that was rather tame by today's standards. (Courtesy the Dallas Cowboys**.**)

CHARLEY BRITT. Another football standout at North Augusta High School was Charley Britt. He became a star player as quarterback at the University of Georgia before playing for the Los Angeles Rams (1960–1963), Minnesota Vikings (1964), and San Francisco 49ers (1964). He was teen rock idol Ricky Nelson's roommate in Los Angeles and made several appearances on *Ozzie & Harriet,* the Nelson family television series. He came home and joined WRDW television, Channel 12, as the sports anchor in 1976. He became the news anchor in 1977. (Courtesy *The Augusta Chronicle.*)

HERSCHEL WALKER. Running as fast as the wind here on November 1, 1980, is Augusta native Herschel Walker of Wrightsville, Georgia, who won the coveted Heisman Memorial Trophy in 1982 while playing for the University of Georgia. He played football and ran track for Johnson County High School in Wrightsville, Georgia. He left the University of Georgia briefly to play for the New Jersey Generals of the United States Football League but returned to complete his bachelor of science degree in criminal justice. He then played 12 seasons with the National Football League with the Dallas Cowboys, Minnesota Vikings, Philadelphia Eagles, and New York Giants. (Photo by Phillip Powell; Courtesy *The Augusta Chronicle*.)

EMERSON BOOZER. This future running back for the New York Jets was born July 4, 1943, at his home in Richmond County. His mom and dad both worked, but their total take-home pay was only $37 per week. Boozer would play football for Lucy Laney High School in Augusta before eventually earning a Super Bowl III championship ring in 1969. He is, at the time of this publication, director of parks and recreation for the town supervisor in Huntington, Long Island, New York. (Courtesy *The Augusta Chronicle*.)

AIKEN STEEPLECHASE. One of the greatest Augusta-area sporting attractions each year is the Aiken Triple Crown, consisting of the Aiken Trials (straight out racing), harness racing, and the steeplechase. Here Vincent Marzullo leads the jumping pack on Leandro, a horse from Chile, to win the third race of the steeplechase on March 26, 1994. (Photo by Ron Cockerille; Courtesy *The Augusta Chronicle*.)

DOG SHOW. The Georgia Society for the Prevention of Cruelty to Animals was founded in Augusta by Louise W. King, daughter of Augusta textile mills owner John P. King. The first official dog show in Augusta was February 22–23, 1924, at the Armory with more than 50 dogs entered. The 61st All-Breed Dog Show, hosted in November of 1987 by the Augusta Kennel Club, saw 995 dogs of 109 different breeds entered. Dr. Robert Smith, judge, here looks over Anna, an Afghan hound shown by Scarlett Highfield. Anna won Winner's Bitch, Best of Winners, and Best of Breed. (Photo by Eric Olig; Courtesy *The Augusta Chronicle*.)

THE AUGUSTA FUTURITY. The opening of the Augusta-Richmond County Civic Center on December 5, 1979, led to the creation of one of its most enduring events. The Atlantic Coast Cutting (Horse) Futurity, later renamed the Augusta Futurity, was first held February 7–9, 1980. It evolved into the largest cutting event east of the Mississippi River. Here, on January 30, 1993, is Helen Groves, who became the Four-Year-Old Non-Pro champion riding Haidas Lorri. (Photo by Jeff Barnes; Courtesy Morris Communications Co.)

BARREL RACING CHAMPIONSHIPS. The National Barrel Horse Association became the first nationwide organization for the barrel horse racing industry when created in Augusta on August 5, 1992. The first NBHA "National Finals"—later renamed the World Championships—was held October 8–16, 1993, in the Augusta-Richmond County Civic Center, with qualifiers coming from almost every state. Here in 1995, Justin Hayworth of Rensselaer, Indiana, rides Thini to win the Youth Second Division championship. (Photo by Eric Olig; Courtesy Morris Communications Co.)

RAFT RACE. Thousands of Augusta area water lovers over the years took part in the many raft races on the Savannah River. Here scores of rafters prepare to launch their crafts near the Old Lock and Dam on August 18, 1990. (Photo by Eric Olig; Courtesy *The Augusta Chronicle*.)

DAM DEDICATION. The dedication of the $2 million New Savannah River Lock & Dam was a cause of great celebration in Augusta on June 26, 1937. VIP guests were transported on a boat from the Fifth Street dock to the new lock and dam downriver in a slow journey that took two leisurely hours. Boats and by-standers waved to the VIPs along the way. (Photo by John Barnes; Courtesy *The Augusta Chronicle*.)

BOAT RACE, 1837. Augusta's first official boat race took place July 19, 1837, on the Savannah River. About one-third of the city's population watched the *Minerva, Pioneer,* and *Red Michael* compete for two silver cups and a serving tray. The three boats raced from the lower bridge (Fifth Street) to the upper bridge (about Thirteenth Street) and back down the river. The *Minerva* was the victor with a time of 23.5 minutes. (Drawing by Phill Flanders; Courtesy *The Augusta Chronicle.*)

MAPPING THE COURSE. The Augusta Riverfront Marina was created specifically for the first Augusta Invitational Rowing Regatta. It was held April 7, 1984, on the Savannah River with 13 participating collegiate teams. It marked one of the first times in many years the Savannah River south of Fifth Street had been used for recreational competitions. Here on November 12, 1983, the regatta course was mapped out by, from left to right, Augusta Port Authority chairman Duncan Wheale, U.S. Rowing Association representative Bill Jurgens, Port Authority vice chairman Tom Harley, and national rowing official Norman Schlachter. (Photo by Mark Phillips; Courtesy *The Augusta Chronicle.*)

RACING ON THE SAVANNAH. River Race Augusta competitors in the first SST 120 qualifying heat on June 11, 1994, head down the straightaway to the first turn on the Savannah River course. The river, basically ignored in the 1950s and 1960s, was revived for recreational uses in the 1970s with the creation of the Augusta Riverfront Marina, whose funding was arranged by Augusta mayor Edward M. McIntyre. (Photo by Blake Madden; Courtesy *The Augusta Chronicle*.)

Soap Box Derby Racers. Tracy Carter, left, and Steven Sullivan look at soap box racing cars on display at Harrison- Gulley Chevrolet on July 8, 1976. Note the Soap Box Derby registration booth at back right. The race itself was held July 10 at Fort Gordon Derby Downs. Local champions were sent to the national finals at Akron, Ohio. (Photo by Lee Downing; Courtesy *The Augusta Chronicle*.)

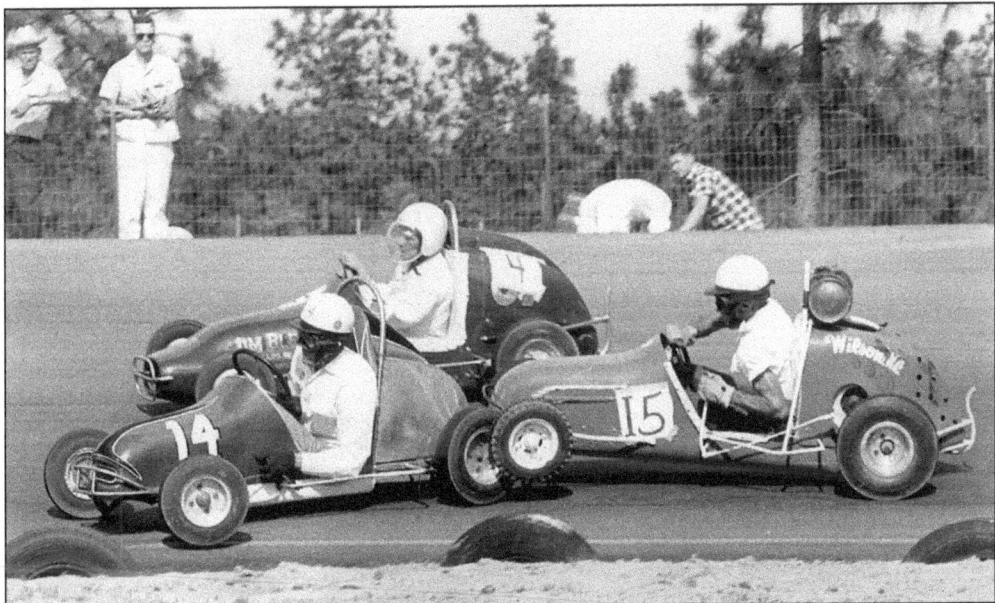

Small Racers at Speedway. Not all race cars have to be big, powerful vehicles for racing fun, as these small fry proved on June 4, 1962, at the International Speedway in Richmond County. Frank Jarrell of Mt. Airy, North Carolina, in car number 14 won the National Micro Midget Industrial Flathead division championship. (Photo by Al Ludwick; Courtesy *The Augusta Chronicle*.)

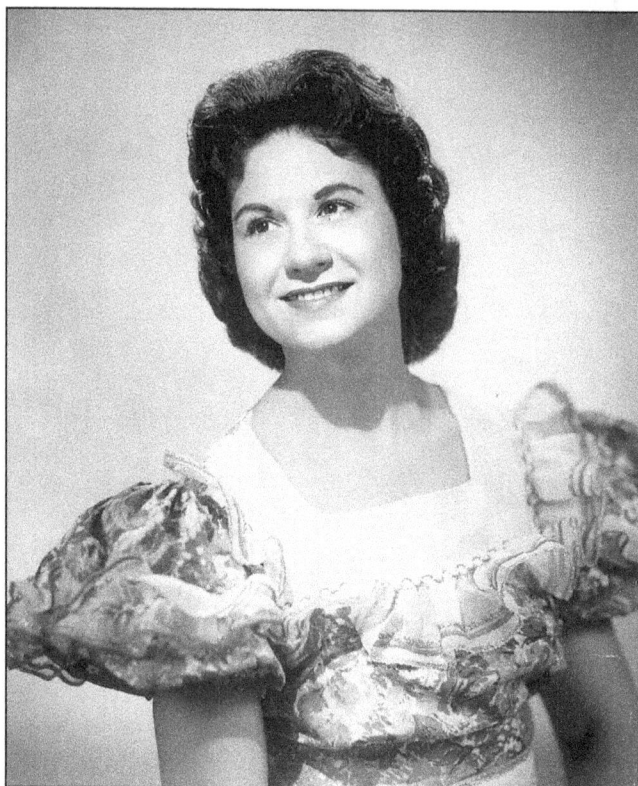

KITTY WELLS. The "Queen of Country Music" has entertained Augusta area fans many times. They include performing with Little Jimmy Dickens, Shot Jackson, Claude Casey, and Johnny Wright (her husband) and his partner Jack Anglin in Bell Auditorium on October 4, 1953, and with Lester Flatt and Earl Scruggs, Ray Pillow, Bill Phillips, and her husband in the Bell on July 18, 1964. (Courtesy Decca Records.)

STEVE CHAPPELL. The first and, as of this writing, only Georgian to win the annual major "Images of the King" (Elvis impersonation) contest in Memphis, Tennessee, is Steve Chappell of Augusta, who beat out finalists from across the nation in 1994. Chappell was introduced to Presley's music by his uncle, Jerry Chappell, and on his sixth birthday, received the *Girls, Girls, Girls* Presley album from his mother. (Courtesy Steve Chappell.)

Seven

THE STARS SHINE BRIGHT

Nationally-known actor Thomas Apthorpe Cooper apparently was the first "celebrity" to entertain Augustans with his performances February 24–March 4, 1820.

Down through the years afterward, Augusta has been visited by many famous stage actors, vaudeville performers, movie stars, and music legends in town for a performance, visit, or sporting event.

Among them have been adventure heroes such as Tim McCoy, Johnny Mack Brown, Tex Ritter, Gene Autry, Lassie, The Lone Ranger, and Tarzan; musicians such as Louis Armstrong, Count Basie, and Paul Whiteman; lecturers such as Oscar Wilde, Carrie Nation, and Booker T. Washington; dancers such as the Ziegfield Follies, George M. Cohan, and Anna Pavlowa; vocalists such as Marian Anderson, Ella Fitzgerald, and Bill Monroe; comedians such as Bob Hope, Minnie Pearl, and Jay Leno; and movie stars such as Tyrone Power, Tallulah Bankhead, and the Good Witch of the North herself, Billie Burke.

They paved the way for the myriad of superstars who have followed.

STRINGS AND SYMPHONY. The Savannah River Strings bluegrass band rehearses on November 10, 1980, for a guest appearance with the Augusta Symphony. Strings members shown are, from left to right, guitarist Henry Wynn, banjoist Bobby Lovett, and upright bass player Warren Twiggs. (Photo by Chuck Bigger; Courtesy *The Augusta Chronicle.*)

AUGUSTA SEA BEACH. Two popular entertainment venues for African-American citizens in the Central Savannah River Area in the 1930s and 1940s were Palmetto Pond near North Augusta, South Carolina, and Augusta Sea Beach (shown here) in south Richmond County. Augustan Arthur Lee Simpkins and his Night Hawks band were frequent performers at Augusta Sea Beach on Butler Creek off Old Savannah Road (Highway 56). Big name entertainers there also included Fats Waller, Count Basie, King Joe Oliver, and Tiny Bradshaw. The resort closed in late 1940. (Courtesy the Augusta Museum of History.)

THE PANTOMITES. Tommy Hodges, top, and Robert Symms in the 1950s were the Pantomites, an Augusta comedy duo who cheered up local nightlife patrons. They left Augusta in March of 1952 to join USO Camp Shows Inc. for a three-month tour entertaining soldiers in Japan, Korea, and the Pacific islands. The team didn't last but their friendship did, with popular pianist Hodges becoming known as "Mr. Tom Cat" and Symms becoming co-owner with Morgan Fitz of Fitz-Symms photography studio. This photo was taken at Augusta's old Union train station. (Courtesy Fitz-Symms Studio.)

COUNTRY ROYALTY. Three of country music's most award-winning artists—(left to right) Hank Williams Jr., George Jones, and his then wife Tammy Wynette—gathered on a touring bus parked next to Bell Auditorium where the three performed two shows the same day on January 17, 1972. Also in the two shows were Dolly Parton, Porter Wagoner, and Faron Young. (Photo by Nelson Harris; Courtesy *The Augusta Chronicle*.)

DOLLY AND PORTER. One of the most famous duet teams in country music history with 21 hit singles was Dolly Parton and Porter Wagoner (shown in Bell Auditorium during their appearance on January 17, 1972). Their split just two years later was bitter, with Parton writing her classic "I Will Always Love You" about Wagoner. Years later, they would renew their friendship, which resulted in 2002 with Parton singing "I Will Always Love You" on the Grand Ole Opry House stage with Vince Gill while Wagoner stood a few feet away. (Photo by Nelson Harris; Courtesy *The Augusta Chronicle*.)

TEX RITTER. Movie and singing star Tex Ritter was in Augusta in mid-December of 1972 to perform in the Country Carrousel club on Broad Street. Shown here, from left to right, are Ritter, Augusta mayor Lewis A. Newman, and Augusta police chief James Beck. Other Augusta appearances for Ritter, father of television star John Ritter, included August 26, 1945, in Municipal (later Bell) Auditorium and January 10–11, 1949, in the Modjeska Theater with his horse, White Flash. (Photo by Jimmy Watkins; Courtesy *The Augusta Chronicle*.)

GENE AUTRY. Western movie and singing legend Gene Autry was in Augusta for two shows on January 21, 1948, in the Municipal Auditorium with his horse, Champion, and his Melody Ranch radio show cast members (Pat Buttram, Johnny Bond, and others). He was back for two more shows in the auditorium on March 3, 1950, with 40 entertainers and his horses, Champion and Little Champ. His troupe arrived the day before. Autry on the day of the show piloted his twin-engine Beechcraft into Daniel Field airport. He was in the last week of performing in 68 cities in 70 days. Champion on the second trip to town made a personal appearance in the boy's department of White's department store on Broad Street. (Courtesy *The Augusta Chronicle*.)

PIANO DUO. Pianists Artemisia Thevaos, left, and Cuban-born Lydia Porro Milham, photographed here on March 29, 1981, have been two of Augusta's most popular classical musicians over the past 40 years. The duo first performed together at Indiana University in the 1950s. Their first local concert was May 3, 1962, for a luncheon meeting of the Augusta Exchange Club. (Photo by Lannis Waters; Courtesy *The Augusta Chronicle*.)

AUGUSTA RADIO STARS. Ramblin' Tommy Scott of Toccoa, Georgia, who crisscrossed America and Canada for decades with his Old Time Medicine Show, center, is flanked by Grand Ole Opry stars Jesse McReynolds, left, and his brother, Jim McReynolds. Scott performed in Augusta live on WRDW radio in Augusta with Curley Seckler (later a member of Flatt and Scruggs' Foggy Mountain Boys.) The McReynolds brothers, who became stars on the *Grand Ole Opry*, performed live on WGAC radio. The trio reunited on May 4, 2000, at the Lewis Family's Homecoming and Bluegrass Festival at Elijah Clark State Park. Jim McReynolds would die two years later of cancer at age 75 on December 31, 2002. (Courtesy Tommy Scott.)

LIBERACE. Making several clothing changes in Bell Auditorium on November 23, 1965, was the famous pianist Liberace, shown here displaying his piano-shaped wristwatch to Mrs. Charles Royal. The headliner in the Famous Artist Series presented by the Augusta Junior Woman's Club also delighted the audience by playing a medley of Georgia songs. (Breault Newsfoto; Courtesy *The Augusta Chronicle*.)

BOB HOPE. For his first visit to Augusta, Bob Hope's plane had to land at the Aiken, South Carolina airport, where he was met by Augusta mayor W.D. Jennings. That January 19, 1949, appearance in Municipal Auditorium was with his "big 2-hour Hollywood Stage Show," which included Doris Day, Les Brown and his band, and Irene Ryan (later Granny on *The Beverly Hillbillies*). He was back in Augusta June 7–10, 1972, to visit with the family of Dr. Robert Greenblatt, whose son, Nathaniel, was then married to Hope's daughter, Linda. This photo shows Dr. Greenblatt's daughter, Deborah, left, with Bob and Dolores Hope. (Photo by John Drummond; Courtesy *The Augusta Chronicle*.)

EDGAR BERGEN. The famous ventriloquist and father of *Murphy Brown* actress Candace Bergen was in Bell Auditorium on November 23, 1973, with his famous puppet friends Mortimer Snerd (shown here) and Charlie McCarthy. (Photo by Jimmy Watkins; Courtesy *The Augusta Chronicle*.)

RED SKELTON. Movie and television series comedian Red Skelton spent four days in Augusta in mid-May of 1982 rehearsing for the concert with the Augusta Symphony in the Civic Center on May 15. He recalled performing in Augusta many years earlier with the Hagenbeck-Wallace Circus and also another time with a medicine show. He gave reporters some insight into his life, saying, "After a concert is over, and I have signed autographs and the people have left, I walk out and see the empty seats. I don't hear the laughter. I don't hear any applause, and I become myself again." (Photo by Michael Lewis; Courtesy *The Augusta Chronicle*.)

THE LEGENDS PERFORM. Clockwise from the top left are advertisements for performances by Cab Calloway, May 21, 1941; Duke Ellington, December 12, 1947; Louis Armstrong, December 24, 1942; Ethel Waters, May 13, 1922; and Fats Waller, February 23, 1941.

B.B. KING. Famous blues guitarist B.B. King brought his guitar, "Lucille," to Bell Auditorium on June 12, 1991. He had been in the Bell earlier on February 9, 1961, with Sam Cooke, Etta James, Ben E. King, Joe Tex, Gary U.S. Bonds, and The Vibrations. (Photo by Blake Madden; Courtesy *The Augusta Chronicle*.)

NAOMI AND WYNONNA JUDD. Naomi Judd, left, and her daughter, Wynonna, performed in the Augusta-Richmond County Civic Center on October 24, 1991. Their first area appearance actually was outdoors at Uncle Tom's Farm near Edgefield, South Carolina, on June 28, 1985. Naomi also would return to Augusta on May 30, 1995, for the Celebrating Women Conference in the Radisson Riverfront Hotel sponsored by St. Joseph's Hospital's Women's Health Services. (Photo by Walt Unks; Courtesy *The Augusta Chronicle*.)

CASEY JENKINS. It was always a fun time when you were around Casey Jenkins, general manager of WGUS country music radio station in North Augusta. Here he hosts the WGUS Country Jam in Bell Auditorium on March 8, 1981. Jenkins was so beloved that when he died October 10, 1982, there were two memorial services, both heavily attended: one in Augusta and one in Nashville, where he was buried. (Photo by George Schaeffer; Courtesy Casey Jenkins.)

WEBB PIERCE. Inducted into the Country Music Association's Hall of Fame in 2001, Pierce performed in Augusta several times, including April 4, 1952, in Bell Auditorium with Carl Smith, Claude Casey, and Peanut Faircloth. He had more than just a passing interest in the area; he owned three local radio stations managed by his old friend Johnnie Bailes. Pierce was selling men's shirts at the Sears store in Shreveport, Louisiana, when Bailes (then lead vocalist with the Bailes Brothers) got Pierce hired as a member of the popular *Louisiana Hayride* show. (Courtesy Decca Records.)

ALABAMA. The country superstar band Alabama originally came to Augusta as Wild Country, backing up *Grand Ole Opry* star Ray Pillow for a concert in Bell Auditorium. They came back later to pack the Civic Center. Their press conference at the then–Augusta Hilton (now Ramada) on March 13, 1984, found Jeff Cook, center, telling a fishing story flanked by laughing fellow band members Teddy Gentry, left, and Randy Owen. Not seen is fourth band member, drummer Mark Herndon. (Courtesy *The Augusta Chronicle*.)

OSMOND BROTHERS AND MARIE. Marie Osmond, center, is surrounded by her brothers, Alan, left, and Merrill at a press conference on April 4, 1986, in Augusta at the Medical College of Georgia (MCG). The famous family act was at MCG to promote their concert at the Etherredge Center in Aiken, South Carolina, benefiting MCG's Children's Medical Center. (Photo by Lannis Waters; Courtesy *The Augusta Chronicle*.)

GARTH BROOKS. Country music superstar Garth Brooks, shown in one of his first publicity photos, electrified a capacity crowd at the Riverwalk Amphitheater in Augusta on September 28, 1990. Tickets were $20 for reserved seats and $12 for general admission, with proceeds benefiting the Medical College of Georgia's Project Wish program for children with cancer and serious blood diseases. Brooks and members of his band worked off some energy at their sound check the afternoon of the show by running up and down the amphitheater steps. He got from his bus, parked on the south side of the levee, to the amphitheater stage on the north side by riding a golf cart along the lower Riverwalk walkway. (Courtesy Capitol Records.)

PATSY CLINE. This legendary singer performed in Bell Auditorium on November 21, 1959, opening a show for Faron Young. Also opening for Young were Roy Drusky and Carl Bellew. Tickets were $1.10 bought in advance for adults or 60¢ for servicemen and children 12 and younger. One year later on November 16, 1960, Cline would record her career-making record *I Fall To Pieces*. (Courtesy Decca Records.)

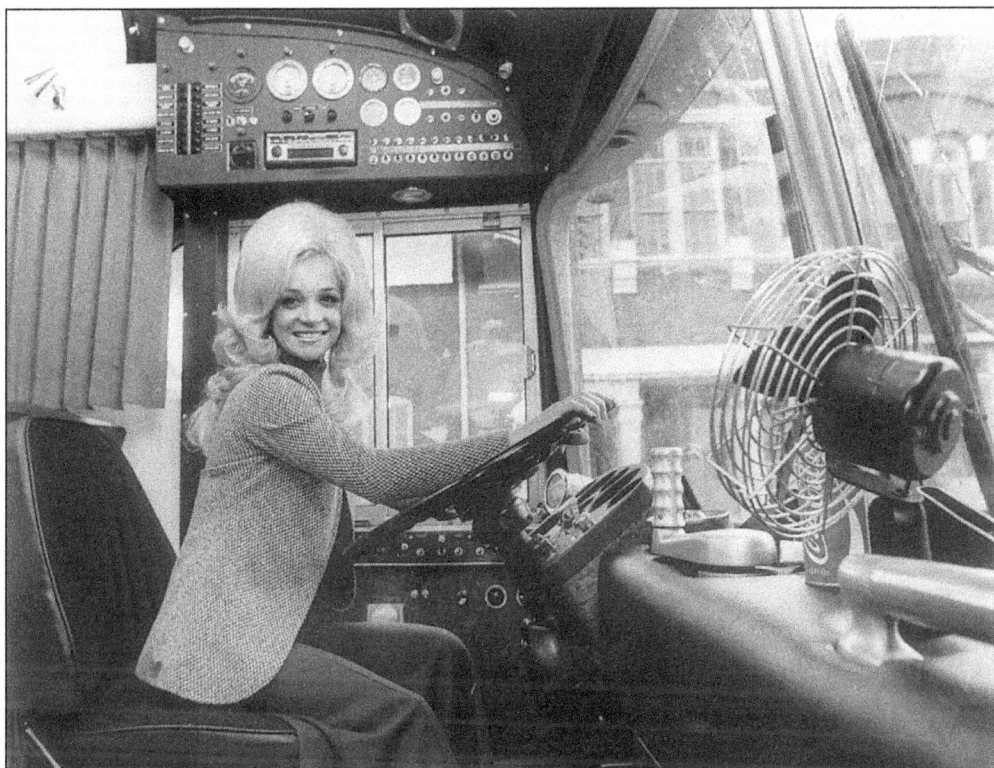

BARBARA MANDRELL: Frequent Augusta visitor Barbara Mandrell in June of 1973 showed off her brand new, custom-made touring bus parked in front of the Country Carousel nightclub on Broad Street, where she was performing three shows a night for a week. The governor of Tennessee, a short time earlier, had cut a ribbon across the door of the bus in a dedicatory ceremony in Nashville. (Photo by Jim King; Courtesy *The Augusta Chronicle*.)

LORETTA LYNN. Another repeated Augusta visitor has been Loretta Lynn, "the coal miner's daughter." She joined Ernest Tubb, Claude King, and Audrey Williams in opening for Hank Williams Jr. in Bell Auditorium on November 12, 1965. This photo of her in the doorway of her touring bus was taken when she returned for a concert in Bell Auditorium on February 23, 1975. Lynn did several concerts in the Bell with and without her often duet partner, Conway Twitty. (Photo by Mike Claven; Courtesy *The Augusta Chronicle*.)

DIANA ROSS. The Supremes apparently never came to Augusta, but Diana Ross performed in the round in the Civic Center to a sold-out crowd on March 5, 1983. One highlight of her concert was when she walked high up the Civic Center steps and sang "Why Do Fools Fall In Love?" with five-year-old Rasheda Downs. (Photo by Drake White; Courtesy *The Augusta Chronicle*.)

JOHNNY CASH. The "Man in Black" signed an autograph for 89-year-old Lula Mayson of North Augusta in Bell Auditorium on February 15, 1977. Cash had just met her backstage. He later had the house lights turned up during his concert, recognized her in the audience, and sang "Peace In The Valley" after dedicating it to her. Performing with Cash in the Bell that night were his wife, June Carter, who had performed in the Bell on March 20, 1956, opening for Elvis Presley, and also his brother, singer Tommy Cash. (Photo by Bill Middleton; Courtesy *The Augusta Chronicle*.)

LYNN ANDERSON. Country music superstar Lynn Anderson greeted fans from horseback in the Civic Center in January of 1993 during the celebrity competition at the Augusta Futurity. She also interviewed other celebrity cutters from horseback using a wireless microphone. The Grammy Award winner (for "Rose Garden") earlier had performed next door in Bell Auditorium on April 30, 1978, for a show benefiting the Lynndale School and Training Center. (Photo by Wingate Downs; Courtesy Morris Communications Co.)

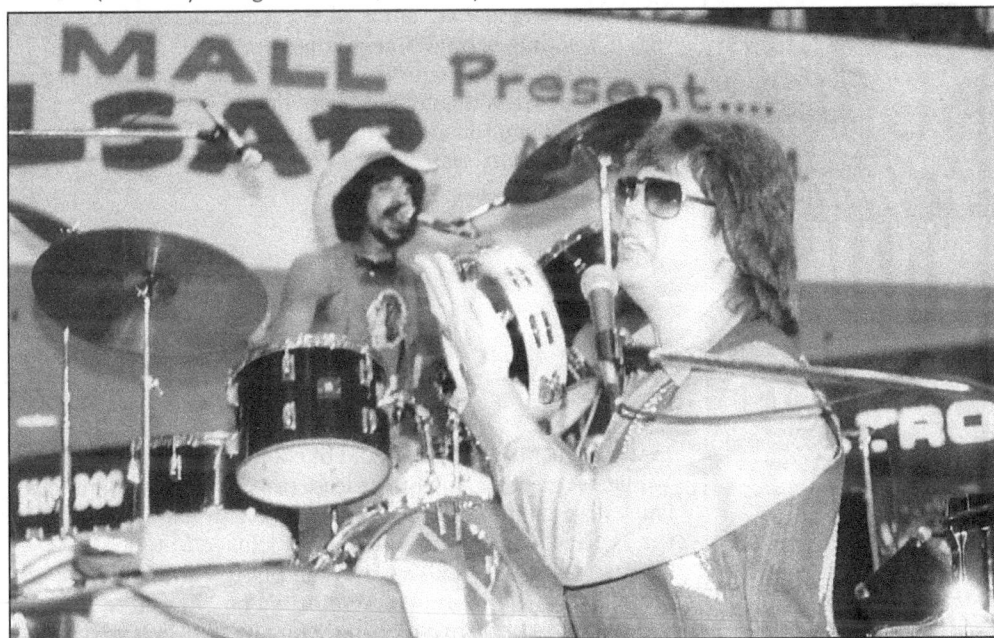

RONNIE MILSAP. When Regency Mall was in its heyday, celebrities were hired by mall management to perform free concerts there to attract shoppers. One was Ronnie Milsap, 1977 Country Music Association Entertainer of the Year, who thrilled an enormous crowd estimated at 20,000 on April 29, 1979. (Photo by John Sorrells; Courtesy *The Augusta Chronicle*.)

GUNTHER GEBEL-WILLIAMS. The greatest of all circus performers, Gunther Gebel-Williams, came to Augusta several times with the Ringling Bros. and Barnum & Bailey Circus, including this appearance in the Civic Center on February 1, 1980. He was a master trainer of elephants, horses, lions and tigers. Standing behind him are his wife, Sigrid, and his son, Mark Oliver, who took over when his father officially retired in 1990. Gebel-Williams had never missed one of his more than 12,000 performances. (Photo by Phillip Powell; Courtesy *The Augusta Chronicle*.)

HANK WILLIAMS. The lost soul of country music, Hank Williams, came to Augusta at least twice. He was in Jennings baseball stadium on Walton Way on August 25, 1951, with the Hadacol Caravan tour that also included Minnie Pearl, Carmen Miranda, Jack Dempsey, and Dick Haymes. He returned to perform in Bell Auditorium on November 16, 1952, just less than two months before he died on the night of December 31, 1952. His son, Hank Jr., who really wasn't a junior, later would perform in both Bell Auditorium and the Augusta-Richmond County Civic Center. (Courtesy *The Augusta Chronicle*.)

Reba McEntire. Another singing superstar who has made repeated trips to Augusta is Reba McEntire. McEntire is shown here visiting on February 19, 1988, with Julie Charron, seven-year-old poster child for the burn unit at Humana (later re-changed to Doctor's) Hospital, and Dr. Joseph Still, director of the burn unit. (Photo by Rudy Nyhoff; Courtesy *The Augusta Chronicle.*)

Willie Nelson. Pouring his heart and soul into his music to about 3,000 fans at Augusta Riverfront Marina on May 14, 1989, was Willie Nelson. The concert almost didn't come off that day because the promoter lacked the contracted pre-show payment. (Photo by Blake Madden; Courtesy *The Augusta Chronicle.*)

ELVIS ARRIVES. The nation's biggest rock sensation arrived at the backstage door of Bell Auditorium on June 27, 1956, for his second Augusta appearance. Waiting inside the 5,000-seat building on both the Music Hall and Main Auditorium sides of the common stage were 6,000 fans taking up every available viewing space. He had performed to a smaller-sized crowd in Bell Auditorium three months earlier on March 20. Johnny Cash's future wife, June Carter, and her mother, Maybelle, were his opening acts for that show, along with *Grand Ole Opry* comedian Rod Brasfield. (Photo by Robert Symms; Courtesy Fitz-Symms Studio.)

GREETING FANS. Two local singers, Mercia Carr, left, and Margie Walker, were able to get close to the king of rock and roll during his June 27 appearance. So did young Augustans Louise Cowart and Melvis Broadwater. Cowart, then 12, had been picked by the *Augusta Herald* as an average fan to greet the rising legend. She asked nearby neighbor Melvis, then 15, to be her escort. Melvis told Elvis that they shared the same birthday—January 8. (Photo by Robert Symms; Courtesy Fitz-Symms Studio.)

Eight

THE RISE OF
ROCK AND ROLL

Rock and roll was born out of gospel, country, jazz, swing, and blues, out of music that stirred listeners' souls and caused them to snap their fingers and move their feet and other body parts.

Jitterbug contests were being held at places like the Delmar Casino on Ninth Street in August of 1945, and Snookum Russell and his Reet Band were at Catholic Hall in October of that year. Standing outside the Delmar Casino, listening to the soulful rockin' sounds inside of Louis Jordan was young Augustan James Brown.

Meanwhile on April 26, 1949, rock and roll pioneer Wynonie "Mr. Blues" Harris was singing "Good Rocking Blues" and "Good Rocking Tonight" in the Harlem Theatre.

But nothing, absolutely nothing, rocked Augustans as when 6,000 music fans packed 5,000-seat Bell Auditorium to watch the second Augusta appearance of Elvis Presley on June 27, 1956.

ELVIS ONSTAGE. Opening with his first RCA single, "Heartbreak Hotel," and closing with his soon-to-be-released "Hound Dog," Elvis Presley rips up the Bell stage with guitarist Scotty Moore and drummer D.J. Fontana. Not seen is upright bass fiddle player Bill Black. (Photo by Hugh Pinney; Courtesy Fitz-Symms Studio.)

JOHNNY HENSLEY AND THE RED HOTS. One of the earliest rockin' bands in Augusta in the 1950s was the Red Hots led by vocalist Johnny Hensley. Pictured here are, from left to right, (front row) Johnny Dixon, Wayne Dinkins, and Johnny Hensley; (middle row) Steve Davidowski, Billy Walker, and Robert Kitchens; (back row) drummer Art Greene. Hensley in the 1960s also led the Celestials, which became the house band at the Whisk-A-Go-Go nightclub on Broad Street and which opened for Roy Orbison in Bell Auditorium on July 1, 1961. Hensley (with partner Frank Mears) booked major acts into the Bell in the 1960s and 1970s. He also once booked unknown Otis Redding into the Garden Center on Telfair Street for $325. (Courtesy Johnny Hensley.)

JERRY LEE LEWIS. "The Killer," Jerry Lee Lewis, then 22, greeted fans in Bell Auditorium on June 27, 1958. He had been advertised to appear with his 13-year-old bride, but she stayed behind in Atlanta due to car trouble. His other Bell appearances included November 10, 1957, with Webb Pierce, Kitty Wells, Johnny & Jack, and Warner Mack and also on November 18, 1961, with Charlie Rich and Bobby Sheridan. (Photo by Morgan Fitz; Courtesy Fitz-Symms Studio.)

ALLYN LEE AND FRIENDS. One of Augusta's best storytellers and most interesting people is Allyn Lee, who booked major artists such as Jackie Wilson, left, and James Brown, right, into Bell Auditorium in the early 1960s while working for WTHB radio. He also became a popular disc jockey and show promoter in the late 1960s in Montgomery, Alabama, where one of his friends was a pastor whose church was across the street: Martin Luther King Jr. (Courtesy Allyn Lee.)

KENNY ROGERS. Future country music superstar Kenny Rogers still was fronting his soft rock band, the First Edition, when they performed nightly for a week (August 19–24, 1974) at Leonard's Lounge on Dean's Bridge Road. Playing touch football near their motel one afternoon were Rogers and First Edition members Terry Williams, center, and Mary Arnold, later married to Roger Miller until his death. (Photo by Jim Watkins; Courtesy *The Augusta Chronicle*.)

THE GEORGIA PROPHETS. One nationally-known band to come out of Augusta in the 1960s was the Georgia Prophets, which was also one of the South's first interracially-mixed rock groups. The band in 1997 was inducted into the Cammy Awards (for beach music acts) Hall of Fame in Charlotte, North Carolina. Members shown in this photo are, from left to right, Moy Harris, Barbara Scott (Goudy), Roy Smith, Janet Helm (Dearstone), Tommy Witcher, Billy Scott, and Fred Williamson. Smith wrote many of the group's hits, including its top seller, "I Got The Fever." (Courtesy *The Augusta Chronicle*.)

DIXIE DREGS. Probably the best-selling band to come out of Augusta was Dixie Grit, which evolved into Dixie Dregs, which evolved into just the Dregs. Augusta musicians Steve Morse and Andy West co-formed Dixie Grit. Shown here, from left to right, are members Allen Sloan, Steve Davidowski, Rod Morgenstein, Steve Morse, and Andy West. Morse later would be named "Best Overall Guitarist" five times in *Guitar Player* magazine's readers' poll. He also later played with the band Kansas and, as of this writing, has been touring with Deep Purple. (Courtesy Capricorn Records.)

CROSSROADS. Another popular Augusta rock band in the early 1970s was Crossroads, which broke up in 1977. It was founded by Georgia Prophets member Tommy Witcher. Pictured here, from left to right, are (front row) Stanley Sherman and Tommy Witcher; (back row) Robbie Ducey and Jimmy Burch. They backed celebrities in local nightclubs, and they once spent five weeks performing at a U.S. Air Force base in Greenland. Ducey later owned and managed West Wind Studios Inc. in Evans, Georgia. (Courtesy Robbie Ducey.)

BARRY MANILOW. Playing a clarinet and singing his pop rock songs in the Civic Center on November 15, 1981, was Barry Manilow. He performed in Jacksonville, Florida, the night before the Augusta show and in Savannah the night afterward. (Photo by Lannis Waters; Courtesy *The Augusta Chronicle*.)

WAYLON JENNINGS. Waylon Jennings, former guitarist for Buddy Holly's band the Crickets, became the first celebrity act in the new, $20 million, 9,500-seat Augusta-Richmond County Civic Center on December 14, 1979. Also part of the show were the Crickets and singer Johnny Rodriguez. The Civic Center had been dedicated on December 5, with U.S. Representative D. Douglas Barnard Jr. giving the keynote speech. The civic center's large size allowed superstar acts to come to Augusta. (Courtesy RCA Records.)

STEWART HARRIS. Shown here, from left to right, are songwriter Jill Colucci, country star Wynonna Judd, and songwriter Stewart Harris. He formed and led the popular Aiken, South Carolina, rock band The Intruders in the late 1960s. His father, Joseph, was headmaster of Aiken's Mead Hall Episcopal Parochial School, where his mother, Rosa, also taught French. Harris wrote such hit singles as Judd's "No One Else On Earth," Travis Tritt's "I'm Gonna Be Somebody" and "Can I Trust You With My Heart?," and Mickey Gilley's "(I Can Take These Lonely Days But I Can't Take These) Lonely Nights" as well as the catchy theme for the ABC television series *America's Funniest Home Videos.* (Courtesy Stewart Harris.)

ARCHIE JORDAN. This guitarist for the Aiken band Intruders spent three months as the only white person in the black beach music group the Tams. He co-formed the popular South Carolina rock band the Cobras. He was born in Augusta's old University Hospital and grew up to write dozens of country, rock, and gospel hits, including "It Was Almost Like A Song," "Let's Take The Long Way Around The World," "Drifter," "It's All I Can Do," "What A Difference You Made In My Life," and "Jesus Is Your Ticket To Heaven." He lived eight years in Metter, Georgia, where he acquired his first guitar, a Roy Rogers plastic model. (Courtesy Archie Jordan.)

ROCKING' TRIO. Sitting in the artist tent at the Day in the Country festival at Augusta Riverfront Marina on May 3, 1987, were three 1960s rockers turned 1970s country stars. They are, from left to right, Freddy Weller (former member of Paul Revere & the Raiders), country rocker Narvel Felts ("Everlasting Love"), and Dickey Lee (who wrote and recorded the 1962 mournful ballad "Patches"). (Photo by Don Rhodes.)

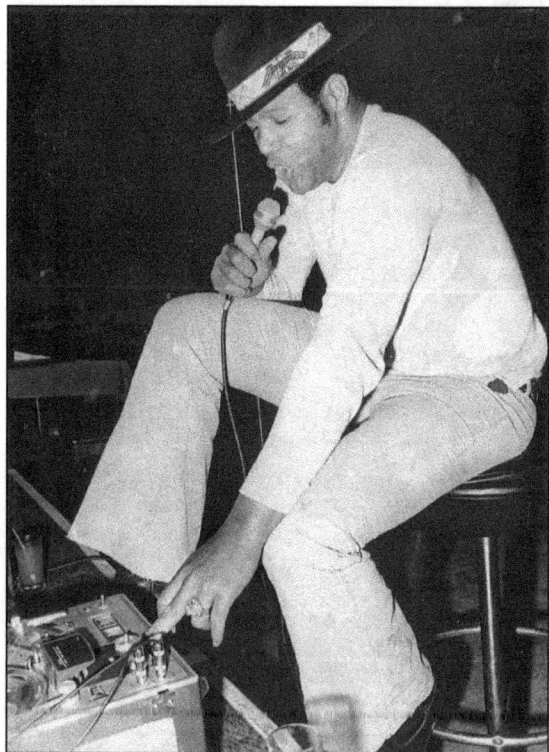

CHUBBY CHECKER. The Twist King himself, Chubby Checker, one of rock music's true originals, rehearsed in the Kitten's Korner nightclub on Dean's Bridge Road (now Martin Luther King Jr. Boulevard) for a week of shows Christmas week of 1971. He ate Christmas Day dinner in Carolina Terrace Apartments in North Augusta with this book's author. Checker actually was born as Ernest Evans on October 3, 1941, in Spring Gulley, South Carolina. (Photo by Nelson Harris; Courtesy *The Augusta Chronicle*.)

SAMMY O'BANION. One of Augusta's most versatile performers for more than 20 years was native Augustan Sammy O'Banion. He grew up hearing pop-music standards on jukeboxes in Luigi's restaurant where his mother was a waitress. His father, a policeman, snuck his under-age son into black nightclubs to hear legends such as Jackie Wilson. Mr. O'Banion led house bands in the 1960s and 1970s at the Cypress Lounge, Kitten's Korner, and Mr. K's in Hornes Motor Lodge. He also hosted the *Heart of the Country* television series that aired in the 1980s on WGAT. He now lives in North Carolina and is lead vocalist with the touring beach music band Mardi Gras. (Photo by Judy Ondrey, Courtesy *The Augusta Chronicle*.)

PEOPLE WHO MUST. Helping create the new wave of Augusta's rock bands has been People Who Must. Shown from left to right are Joe Stevenson, David Milligan, and drummer Joe Gillion rehearsing on July 12, 1990, at an office in Surrey Center. Lead vocalist Stevenson, then 18, wrote all six songs on the band's debut album. The band's name came from a Carl Sandburg poem. (Photo by Mark Dolejs; Courtesy *The Augusta Chronicle*.)

Brief Entertainment Chronology

May 1, 1787	Music teacher Claude Simon presents Augusta's first organized concert at Emanuel Wambersie's house near Bay and Fourth Streets.
May 9–13, 1801	Equestrian circus in town.
June 23, 1808	First known ballet in Augusta performed by Miss Sully, Miss Placide, and Master Placide.
Feb. 24–March 4, 1820	Tragedian actor Thomas Apthorpe Cooper is first entertainment celebrity to perform for Augustans.
December 28, 1849	Opera *La Somnambula* performed.
January 1, 1861	Augusta Choral Society presents first concert.
October 8–9, 1878	Buffalo Bill Cody and his Wild West Show in Girardey's Opera House.
July 6, 1882	Oscar Wilde speaks on Decorative Art in Girardey's Opera House.
January 20, 1895	Edison's Kenetoscope pictures shown in Grand Opera House.
November 3–4, 1904	"Moving Pictures" shown in Grand Opera House.
May 10–11, 1914	Battle scenes of original movie version of *The Littlest Rebel* filmed in Augusta.
February 18, 1918	The Wells (later the Imperial) opens on Broad Street.
April 16, 1918	Charlie Chaplin appears at the Wells to sell Liberty bonds on his 29th birthday.
November 29, 1920	Lenox Theater opens on Ninth Street.
February 22–23, 1924	Augusta Kennel Club holds first dog show in the Armory.
September 10–15, 1928	First all-talking picture, *The Lights of New York*, shown in Modjeska.
July 3, 1930	WRDW radio goes on the air.
January 31, 1940	First showing in Augusta of *Gone With the Wind* in the Imperial.
February 26, 1940	Miller Theater opens on Broad.

March 31, 1940	Municipal (later Bell) Auditorium dedicated.
November 15, 1945	Augusta Players' first production, *Kind Lady,* makes debut in Music Hall section of Bell Auditorium.
November 25, 1953	WJBF-TV goes on the air.
February 14, 1954	WRDW-TV goes on the air.
May 23, 1954	Augusta Civic Orchestra (later Augusta Symphony) debuts in Bell's Music Hall with Harry Jacobs as conductor.
June 14, 1955	First of outside *Evenings in Appleby Garden* events held.
March 20, 1956	Elvis Presley makes first Augusta appearance in Bell Auditorium. He returns on June 27.
September 18, 1957	*Three Faces of Eve,* based on book by two Augusta psychiatrists, has world premiere in Miller Theater.
December 21, 1962	Augusta Civic Ballet's first production, Classical Symphony, held in Bell Auditorium's Music Hall.
September 12, 1966	Georgia PBS station, WCES in Wrens, goes on the air.
September 15, 1967	The Augusta Opera debuts with *La Boheme* in Bell's Music Hall.
February 19, 1968	Greater Augusta Arts Council meets for first time in Aldersgate Methodist Church with Clarence R. Jones selected the first chairman.
Late December, 1968	WATU-TV (later to become WGAT) goes on the air.
December 5, 1979	Augusta-Richmond County Civic Center opens. Waylon Jennings becomes the first celebrity act in the Civic Center on December 14.
October 9–11, 1981	First Arts in the Heart Arts Festival held at Augusta College. Then called Collage '81.
April 7, 1984	First Augusta Invitational Regatta at new Augusta Riverfront Marina.
February 8, 1987	Opening of Sacred Heart Cultural Center.
September 20, 1988	First Tuesday's Music Live concert at St. Paul's Episcopal Church.
June 15, 1990	Grand opening Riverwalk Augusta Amphitheater featuring the Lettermen and Eclipse.
September 24, 1992	Opening preview party of the Morris Museum of Art.
February 6, 1996	Grand opening of the Augusta-Richmond County Museum.
April 20, 1997	Preview party opening Fort Discovery.

BIBLIOGRAPHY

Augusta magazine. Various issues. Augusta, GA: *The Augusta Chronicle.*

AugustaArchives.com electronic archives. Augusta, GA: *The Augusta Chronicle,* (1785–present).

AugustaChronicle.com.

The Augusta Chronicle. Microfilm files; Augusta, GA.

Augusta Herald. Microfilm files; Augusta, GA.

Bell, Earl and Kenneth Crabbe. *The Augusta Chronicle: Indomitable Voice of Dixie, 1785–1960.* Athens, GA: University of Georgia Press, 1960.

Cashin, Edward J. *The Story of Augusta.* Augusta, GA: Richmond County Board of Education, 1980.

Fogleman, Marguerite Flint. *Historical Markers and Monuments of Richmond County, Georgia.* Augusta, GA:Richmond County Historical Society, 1986.

Illustrated Augusta: The City of Opportunities. Augusta, GA: Augusta Federation of Trades, c. 1915.

Kingsbury, Paul, ed. *The Encyclopedia of Country Music.* Oxford, England: Oxford University Press, 1998.

Lee, Joseph M. III. *Augusta: A Postcard History.* Charleston, SC: Arcadia, 1997.

Lee, Joseph M. III. *Augusta and Summerville.* Charleston, SC: Arcadia, 2000.

Montgomery, Erick D., Vickie H. Greene, and Scott W. Loehr. *Augusta Scrapbook: Twentieth Century Memories.* Charleston, SC: Arcadia, 2000.

Rhodes, Don. *Down Country Roads With Ramblin' Rhodes.* Hartwell, GA: North American Publications Inc., 1982.

Rhodes, Don. Individual scrapbooks about Augusta entertainment history.

The Place We Call Home. Augusta, GA: *The Augusta Chronicle,* 1997.

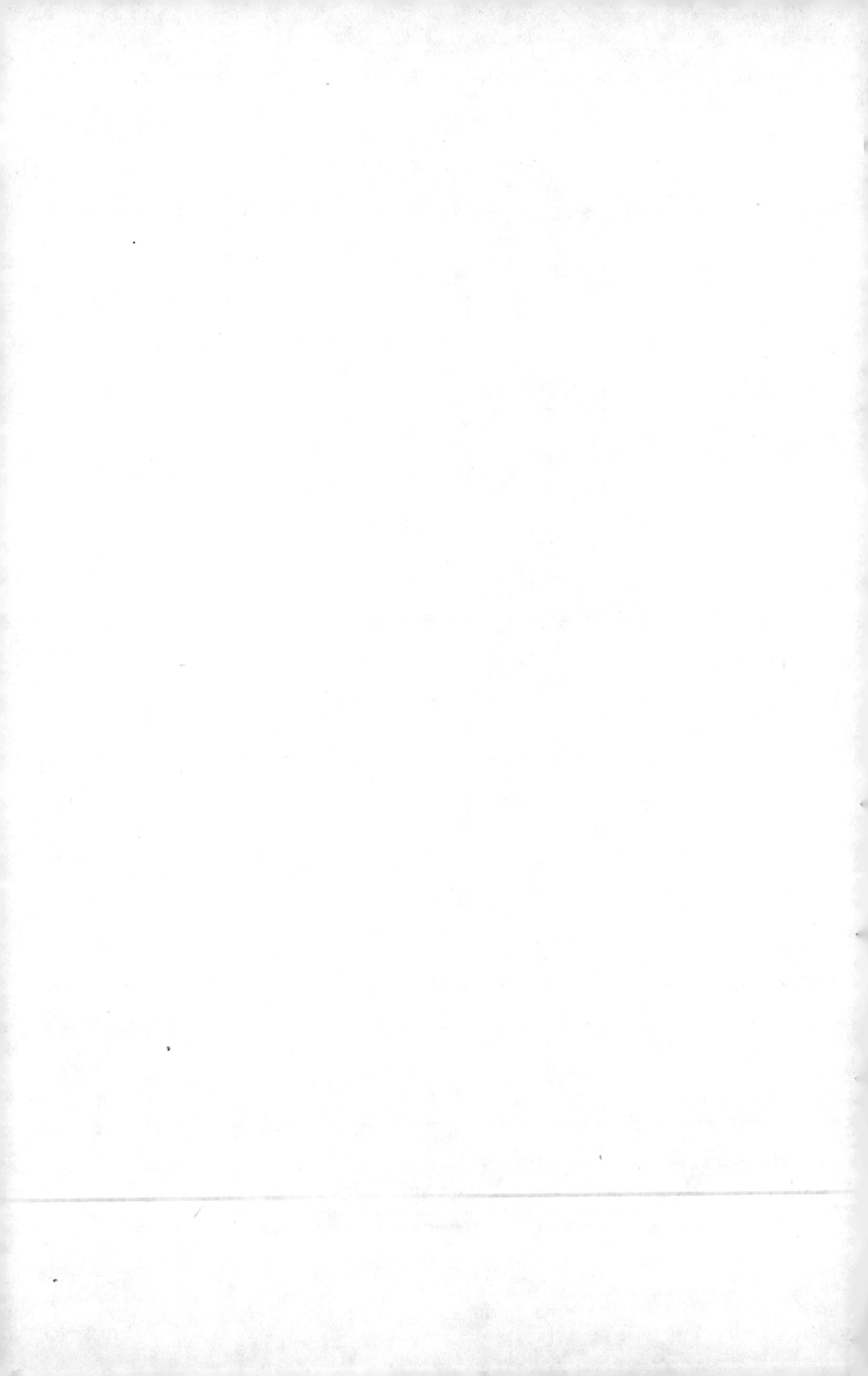